BREATH PERCEPTION

BREATH PERCEPTION

A Daily Guide to Stress Relief, Mindfulness,
and Inner Peace

Barbara Ann Kipfer

Helios
press

Helios Press books may be purchased in bulk at special discounts for sales promotion, corporate gifts, fund-raising, or educational purposes. Special editions can also be created to specifications. For details, contact the Special Sales Department, Helios Press, 307 West 36th Street, 11th Floor, New York, NY 10018 or info@skyhorsepublishing.com.

Helios Press is an imprint of Skyhorse Publishing, Inc.®, a Delaware corporation.

Visit our website at www.skyhorsepublishing.com.

10 9 8 7 6 5 4 3 2

Library of Congress Cataloging-in-Publication Data is available on file.

Interior design by Abigail Gehring
Cover design by Keir Magoulas

Photo credits:
Cover: Keir Magoulas
Author: pages xii, 8, 15, 43, 102, 170, 178, 194, 202, 218, 226, 234, 242, 250, 258, 266, 274, 282, 290
Keir Magoulas: pages 26, 32, 52, 60, 68, 75, 85, 111, 120, 129, 162
James Hatton: pages 94, 210
Kyle Kipfer: page 186

ISBN: 978-1-62914-368-2
Ebook ISBN: 978-1-62914-883-0

Printed in the United States of America

INTRODUCTION

In a fast-paced, technologically driven society, many of us forget to find time to just breathe. *Breath Perception* encourages its readers to slow down and become more mindful. By attaining self-awareness when taking more than 14,000 breaths each day, individuals will soon achieve greater happiness.

Breath Perception offers a guide for understanding the breath and implementing it as an instrument for physical and mental health benefits such as stress relief, higher energy levels, better sleep patterns, improved concentration, and an increased metabolism. In order to heighten the reader's consciousness of breathing, there are 262 simple exercises as well as 104 pieces of wisdom that cover topics ranging from acceptance to Zen. By introducing each technique in a step-by-step manner, *Breath Perception* is easy to follow and serves as a companion to mental, physical, and spiritual development.

The breath is always with you and always "free," but only in the past few years have we started to learn its importance as a mindfulness tool, a concentration help, a meditation focus, and a center of health-giving possibilities. In a similar way, a smile is just a moment away—also free and always possible. We are often reminded by the ubiquitous Thích Nhất Hạnh that smiling and breathing go together. The breath has many lessons to teach us and we are starting to listen. The smile has many gifts to give.

Breath Perception is your companion to understanding the breath and using it as a tool to improve your physical and mental health. Partly because we take the breath for granted and do not "work" with it, we are somewhat unaware of the possibilities to establish proper breathing techniques to address specific needs, such as reducing stress, changing metabolism, and increasing our supply of energy.

Health and Breathing

Breathing is absolutely necessary for animal (and plant) life, but we don't have to think about doing it. Our respiratory system automatically breathes in oxygen from the air, circulates it in the body for burning the food you eat, and then breathes out the carbon dioxide produced. The lungs are the holding area for the oxygen and they release oxygen into the blood vessels. Adults breathe in and out an average of 15 to 20 times per minute, slower when they are sleeping or resting; children may breathe a bit faster than adults. But is that all we need to know?

While automatic breath allows us to survive, we all have acquired unconscious bad habits that restrict or distort the breath, usually as reactions to stress. Breathing affects all bodily systems and even affects sleeping (apnea and snoring), memory and concentration, and energy.

Deep breathing has genuine medical benefits. Slowed, focused breathing can reverse the damaging effects of the f ight-or-f light hormones that f lood the body when you are anxious. Adrenaline and noradrenaline increase heart rate and blood pressure and generate destructive free radicals in the body.

But with each long, deliberate inhale and exhale, you break the train of everyday thought, the fear and the stress of living.

The result is less secretion of stress hormones and more secretion of nitric oxide, which opens the blood vessels, lowering blood pressure. At the same time, metabolism slows down, leading to less free-radical production.

Breath Perception can help you improve the quality of your breathing and even control the state of your breathing. This book has hundreds of alternatives to complicated strategies to address stress, lack of energy, loss of concentration, and poor quality of sleep. You can even address your metabolism and weight through a variety of fairly simple breathing exercises. How? By increasing the amount of oxygen you take in, you help yourself release carbon dioxide and hydrogen more efficiently. This alone reduces the storage of excess fat.

Breath Perception addresses the growing interest in the relationship of breathing to mental, physical, and spiritual development. As you use this book to learn how to sense inner energies and structures of your mind and body, you will make gains in spiritual development and even healing.

Breathing Properly

Many people do not breathe correctly. Knowing how to take a full, deep breath is a true life skill. A full breath cycle spreads life-giving oxygen throughout the body, gets rid of waste gasses like carbon dioxide, and stimulates the spine and internal organs.

Many of us are "chest breathers," meaning we're accustomed to an unhealthy pattern of initiating the breath from the chest. When you fall into a pattern of isolated upper-chest breathing, you overuse muscles in the neck and upper body and underuse the diaphragm. During heavy exercise and in emergency situations, you need those muscles to supplement the diaphragm by getting more air to the lungs. Unlike the diaphragm, the muscles of the neck and upper body tire more easily, leaving you anxious and fatigued.

One of the first steps in learning to breathe well is to learn diaphragmatic deep breathing. When you breath in, the diaphragm contracts and flattens downward creating a vacuum that draws in air. When you exhale, the diaphragm returns to its dome shape, pushing air out of the body.

Once you know how to get your diaphragm working for you, you will find that diaphragmatic breathing is both energizing and relaxing. It is the way a truly efficient body breathes throughout life. Diaphragmatic breathing activates the upper torso yet creates a full, deep pattern of breath.

Lying on your back with your knees bent or straight, put your hands on your lower ribs so that the tips of the middle fingers touch each other at the end of an exhalation. Your shoulders should be relaxed and dropped away from your ears. When you breathe in, try not to let it affect your shoulders. You want your shoulders to stay down and relaxed.

Your spine is long, a neutral spine, a natural position of the spine that allows the curves of the spine to be present. If you are sitting, feel that your weight is falling directly down through your sitting bones and your head is floating up toward the sky. Your throat is open and relaxed.

Breathe in slowly through your nose. Let the air flow into your upper chest and down your spine, expanding your sides and lower ribs, diaphragm, back, and pelvis. Allow the deep inhale to push your belly out a little bit. The chest does move with the breath but remains relaxed and the ribs maintain their cylindrical shape.

Exhale in the reverse order. Drop your lower abdominals, then your belly. Let your ribs pull in, and then let your chest drop as you fully expel all the air. Remain calm and comfortable at all times; never force, and if you feel strain or agitation, stop and let the breath come back to normal.

Learn and practice this breathing before you start reading the book. Practicing this will help you with all of the breathing exercises in the book. Remember that a small smile also helps relax your facial muscles and helps you to breathe fully!

Thank You

Thank you to Skyhorse Publishing for the opportunity to present this material. A big giant thanks to my editor and husband, Paul Magoulas, who performed each exercise to ensure it was understandable and doable and read and edited the manuscript for me. And thank you to Keir Magoulas for the great cover and contribution of photographs to accompany mine in the book.

There are many inspirations in my life, especially my sons Kyle Kipfer and Keir Magoulas, as well as supportive friends and co-workers, like Bob Amsler. Thank you to everyone.

—Barbara Ann Kipfer

About the Author

Barbara Ann Kipfer is the author of more than 50 books, including the bestselling *14,000 Things to Be Happy About* as well as *The Wish List, Instant Karma, 8,789 Words of Wisdom,* and *Self-Meditation*. Barbara has an MPhil and PhD in Linguistics, a PhD in Archaeology, and an MA and PhD in Buddhist Studies. She is a lexicographer. Her websites are www.thingstobehappyabout.com and www.referencewordsmith.com.

Basic breathing meditation

Sit comfortably, whatever that is for you.
Let your eyes close gently.
Invite your body to relax and release into the ground or cushion.
Let go and accept the non-doing of meditation.

Become sensitive to and listen to your breath.
Breathe through your nose.
Feel the air as it goes in and out of the nostrils.
Feel the rising and falling of the chest and abdomen.
Allow your attention to settle where you feel the breath most
    clearly.
Focus there.
Follow the breath.
Allow the breath to be as it is without controlling it.
See the space or pause between breaths.

Thinking will start.
It is a habit.
See each thought like a railroad car of a train going by.
See it, acknowledge it, let it go, and come back to the breath.

It does not matter how many times you get caught up in a thought
    or for how long.
Begin again and bring awareness back to the breath.
This is your practice.
You are strengthening mindfulness.

Awareness of one whole in-breath and one whole out-breath is a
big accomplishment.

If a physical sensation or pain arises, do the same.
See it, acknowledge it without getting caught up by it, let it go,
and come back to the breath.

For 20 minutes, follow your breath with bare attention.
When your mind wanders, stop and come back to the breath.

As you gently open your eyes, try to carry the momentum of your
mindfulness into whatever your next activity may be.

Wake-up call: acceptance

Your aim is to notice the action of your thoughts and to
encourage yourself to accept your wandering mind and
return to your breathing as peacefully as you can.

2

Breath counting

Breath counting is a commonly used practice that harmonizes mind and body. The goal is to keep a mental tally of your breaths without losing count or getting caught up in thoughts.

Sit on a cushion or in a chair, whichever is more comfortable for you, and close your eyes gently.

With your in- and out-breaths, start counting. The simplest method is to inhale and count 1, then exhale and count 2. Count from 1 to 10 and then start again.

You could also try counting a cycle of inhalation and exhalation as 1, then 2, etc.

You might feel frustrated about losing count, so start by doing this for just 5 minutes and then gradually lengthen the time. Remember that you are building your concentration and mindfulness. This is a wonderful way to practice these important qualities.

3

Basic relaxation meditation

Find a comfortable place to lie down on your back, but not
so comfortable that you will likely fall asleep. Your arms lie
slightly out from your sides, palms up. Your legs should be
separate and fall open relaxed. Your eyes should be closed.
Sense your whole body, especially the points where it touches
the surface you are laying on.

Follow your breath at its most noticeable place, perhaps at
your nostrils.

Then bring your awareness to your feet. Wiggle your toes, flex and
relax the feet, letting go of any tension there.

Bring your awareness to your lower legs, slightly tensing the
muscles and then relaxing them.

Do this for your thighs.

Then do this for your hips.

Bring your awareness to your abdomen. Think of the tension
draining away, your abdomen opening and softening. Continue
to follow and observe your breath. Bring your awareness to your
upper abdomen and ribcage, feeling the areas open and soften.

Then do this for your chest and then your neck and throat.

Bring your awareness to your shoulders. Feel their heaviness melting into the surface.

Do this with your upper arms, then the lower arms.

Wiggle your fingers, flex and relax them, letting go of any tension there.

Now bring awareness to your head and face. Feel the tension and then let it melt into the surface.

Feel the calm now in each part of your body. When you scan your body from toe to head and you feel an area of tension, imagine that area relaxing.

When you have scanned your entire body, go back to the breath for 10 more minutes.

Now slowly wiggle your fingers and toes. Begin to stretch your arms and legs. Open your eyes slowly. Gradually come to a sitting position.

Try to carry the momentum of your mindfulness into whatever your next activity may be.

Wake-up call: action

Be awake to the continually changing tones of the breath. Be awake to the blessing of the air flowing in and the air flowing out. Accept each in-breath as the beginning. Accept each out-breath as letting go.

4

Basic walking meditation

Walking meditation is a simple practice. It is learning to be aware as you walk, using the natural movement of walking to cultivate mindfulness and be in the present moment.

Choose a place where you can walk comfortably back and forth, indoors or outdoors—at least 10 to 30 paces in length. You may experiment with the speed on your own, walking at whatever pace keeps you most present. This practice is done for any length of time that you wish.

Begin with your feet firmly planted on the ground. Let your arms and hands rest easily. Close your eyes for a moment, centering yourself, taking a few deep breaths. Feel yourself standing on the earth. Feel the pressure of the bottoms of your feet on the ground. Feel the sensations of standing. Then open your eyes and be present and aware.

Begin to walk slowly. Walk with ease and dignity.

With each step feel all the sensations involved in lifting your foot and leg up from the earth. Be aware as you place each foot back onto the earth.

Relax and let your walking be easy and natural. Be mindful of each step.

Your mind will wander many times, just as in sitting. As soon as you notice this, acknowledge it, then return to feel the next step. Whether your mind has wandered for one second or 10 minutes, simply acknowledge this and come back to being aware of the next step you take.

At the midpoint of your path, pause for a moment. Center yourself and carefully turn around. Pause again so you can be aware of the first step as you walk back.

Walk simply, being truly present for the other half of the walk.

At the end of the path, please pause.

Try to carry the momentum of your mindfulness into whatever your next activity may be.

You can use walking meditation to calm and collect yourself and to live more mindfully in your body. You can extend your walking practice to when you go shopping, whenever you walk down the street, or to or from your car. This practice allows you to enjoy walking for its own sake instead of filling it up with the usual planning and thinking.

Wake-up call: anger management

Befriend your emotions. Befriend your confused or negative emotions. When one arises, like anger, smile to yourself and mentally note, "There's anger again!"

5

Relaxation pose

This is also called corpse pose. You can use a yoga mat, carpeted
  floor, the bed, a couch—anything comfortable for you. You
  might find that having a folded blanket or low pillow under
  your head makes the position more comfortable for your back.

Lie down and close your eyes. Let your legs relax and flop out
  naturally with feet about two feet apart. Arms are also out,
  palms up, and relaxed away from your sides.

Relax your feet, your calves, your thighs, your hips, your buttocks,
  your lower back, your abdomen, your middle and upper
  back, your chest, your shoulders, your arms, your hands, your
  neck. Let your eyes relax into their sockets and feel your facial
  muscles and scalp becoming soft and relaxed.

Mentally scan your body for tension and when you find any,
  tighten the part, then relax it. Allow yourself to melt into the
  floor. Breathe into your abdomen and with each exhalation,
  feel the weight of your body sinking deeper into the floor.

Focus your attention on the breath. Enjoy being supported by the
  floor. If your mind wanders, come back to the breath.

Do this relaxation for at least 5 minutes (10 after a yoga session)
  and then take a deep breath and open your eyes. Come slowly
  up to sitting.

6

ALTERNATE NOSTRIL BREATHING

In a seated position with your eyes closed, press your right middle and index fingers against the palm of your right hand. Press your right thumb to the side of your right nostril as you inhale through your left nostril for 8 counts.

Shut both nostrils using your right thumb on the right side of your nose and your first finger (forefinger) on the left side of your nose and retain the breath. Hold it for as long as comfortable.

Release the thumb and count to 8 as you exhale through your right nostril.

Repeat on the left side. Continue to alternate with one complete inhale/exhale per thumb/forefinger. Do this for 10–20 cycles.

Wake-up call: appreciation of nature

When you are walking in nature, you can smile and say hello to what you see, hear, and come into contact with. Smile at a pebble you happen to step on. Smile at the sky, the trees, the wind. With a smile, you can feel your breath and your steps more clearly.

7

Breath Awareness Exercises

While you are sitting working, you can interweave some breath awareness exercises created by Thích Nhất Hạnh:

Breathing in, I notice I am breathing in. Breathing out, I notice I am breathing out.

Breathing in, I am aware of my body. Breathing out, I calm my body.

Breathing in, I know I am alive. Breathing out, I understand the joy of being alive.

Breathing in, I embrace an unpleasant feeling. Breathing out, I calm that unpleasant feeling.

Breathing in, I look deeply at fear. Breathing out, I liberate myself from fear.

Breathing in, I observe a flower. Breathing out, I contemplate its impermanence.

Breathing in, I look at an object of desire. Breathing out, I see the disappearance of desire.

Repeat for 5 minutes or however long you need to feel peace and awareness.

8

Conscious door opening

As you get ready to leave your home, office, or a room, consciously approach the door.

Take 3 slow deep breaths.

Do you have what you need? Walk out that door and enter the world with your eyes wide open and a smile on your face.

Wake-up call: appreciation of the body

You should strive to gain some measure of control over your basic muscle movements and body functions—fidgeting, nail biting, scratching, and other nervous habits should come under the control of your mind. Normally, you scratch without realizing you itch, seldom noticing the intention that activates the body's movements. What you are seeking to do is to have mindfulness of bodily movements and functions.

9

BREATH FOLLOWING TO MUSIC

Turn on some music that is conducive to sitting and listening. Set it on a continuous loop. Sit in a comfortable position.

Follow your breath while listening to this music—breathing long, light, even breaths while remaining aware of the movement and sentiments of the music. You follow the breath where it is most distinctively felt by you, often at the tip of the nostrils.

Enjoy smooth, relaxing, beautiful music, no words, a gentle instrumental. Use this exercise to take a break from your busy life.

Wake-up call: art

Art is both in the artist and in the work of art—in the one as a cause, in the other as the effect. What is effected is a certain ennoblement of matter, a transformation produced not merely by the hand of the artist, but by his or her thought or knowledge. The arts serve primarily as a medium of spiritual communication. Creating art is a magical form of meditation.

10

SEATED BREATH STRETCHES

To do seated breath stretches, sit in a comfortable position—on a cushion or in a chair.

Close your eyes and concentrate on breathing into the front of your body while raising your arms to the side and over your head, then breathing out, bringing your arms down. This is sun breath.

Then breathe into the back of your body, meaning you will focus your concentration on your back and visualize breathing there, raising your arms over your head. Breathe out, lowering your arms.

Breathe now into the right side of your body, raising your right arm over your head. Breathe out, lowering that arm.

Finally, breathe into the left side of your body, raising your left arm over your head. Breathe out, lowering that arm.

Repeat all four areas 10 times or for a set period of time, maybe 10 minutes.

Atom visualization

In a seated position, close your eyes.

As you inhale, pause to sense and envision the billions of atoms of air soaking into your bloodstream and being carried to nourish and energize every cell and fiber of your body.

As you exhale, pause to envision that through the power of your intent and imagination you imbue the energy bundles of each atom and molecule with your unique blessings.

Envision that each breath is offered as a blessing to the countless beings who are breathing.

Stay with this exercise for 10 minutes or more.

12

KINDNESS BREATHING

You wish to be happy, right? Use your breath to just pay attention and be kind, unconditionally kind, on this breath alone. Take a deep breath in; then breathe out.

Repeat for 5 minutes. This will help you feel kinder and happier.

No matter what the circumstances, just be kind. Everything else will work itself out.

Deep breathing will cleanse you of impurities and realign your being with the energy of prana, the cosmic energy connecting the elements of the universe.

After completing this exercise, take a deep breath and move on in kindness.

13

POINTING AT YOURSELF

Sit in a dark room or alone outside at night. Watch your breath; observe the point where you feel it most strongly. Say, "I will use my finger to point at myself," and then point away in the opposite direction.

Contemplate seeing yourself outside of your bodily form. See yourself in the moon, the air, the universe. Maintain a half-smile and put your hands on your knees, but continue using your mind to point away at yourself, out in the universe. Everyone and everything is connected.

Continue breathing in and out with deep breaths, watching your breath for 10 to 20 minutes.

14

Skull–shining breath

Start by sitting straight and breathing in, expanding your belly.

Exhale by pumping your breath out through your nose, forcefully pulling your belly toward your spine.

Let the in-breath fill your lungs naturally. Repeat the cycle 10–20 times.

Wake-up call: assertion

You may deal with your insecure feelings by creating conflict wherever you go. You see your interactions in terms of power and control. You try to exert control, get your own way, without thinking or caring about others. You may be aggressive or hostile and unaware of how you are perceived. Your speech may be harsh, both in words and tone. You may be abrasive, abusive, aggressive, insensitive—thinking all relationships are struggles in which to assert dominance. You leave a wake of bad feelings. But it does not have to be this way. You can change because it is a matter of choosing a response instead of being carried away by a reaction. Leave a wake of good feelings.

BREATHING DURING COMMERCIALS

When you are watching television, mute the commercials and follow your breathing, grounding your awareness in the present moment. Breathe in and out deeply. Make the act of watching television a little more active.

Alternatively, get up and walk around, look out the window, etc. While walking around the house, follow your breathing. Use the quiet to center yourself.

Wake-up call: attention

Giving attention is one of the purest expressions of love. Awake, reflect, watch, work with care and attention. What do you think is worthy of your attention? What will you give your precious time to? You should be aware of what you are doing and why.

16

MINDFUL DISHWASHING

Practice mindful breathing so the time washing the dishes is pleasant and meaningful. Mindful breathing is focusing on a single, full breath. Notice if you lose focus on that single, full breath and then refocus if necessary.

Do not feel you have to rush or you will waste the time of dishwashing.

While practicing mindful breathing, listen, look, feel, and smell what is around you.

Ask yourself, what am I doing?

This will help you overcome the habit of rushing through tasks and help you focus on the present.

Smile to yourself and say, washing this dish is the most important job in my life.

If your thoughts are carrying you away, you need mindful breathing to intervene.

Use mindful breathing to become more involved with the present moment, especially with activities you often do on auto-pilot. Get into the habit of being aware of everything you do.

17

UJJAYI BREATHING

Sit comfortably. To do ujjayi breathing, inhale deeply through your nose, gently constricting the back of your throat.

Pause briefly at the top of the breath.

Then exhale into your mouth with the mouth closed. Your breath should make a whispering sound like the waves of the ocean or like Darth Vader.

With the mouth closed, continue this practice. Do this for 10–20 cycles.

Wake-up call: awakening

The cultivation of goodness—generosity, patience, faith, and other virtues—is the beginning of spiritual awakening. Awakening is the recovery of that awesome freedom into which you were born. Over time, you develop a false sense of a separate self. Awakening is regaining freedom found in understanding that we are all interconnected and interdependent.

18

DEEPER BREATHING

Try this exercise anytime. Expand your lungs as you inhale and when it feels as though they are at full capacity, gently add in one-tenth more air. Do not force it.

Then exhale and when your lungs feel empty, expel an extra one-tenth of stale air.

By doing this, you are training yourself in diaphragmatic breathing. Diaphragmatic breathing, abdominal breathing, belly breathing, or deep breathing is breathing that is done by contracting the diaphragm, a muscle located horizontally between the chest cavity and stomach cavity. Air enters the lungs and the belly expands during this type of breathing. This deep breathing is marked by expansion of the abdomen rather than the chest when breathing. It is considered by some to be a healthier way to breathe and a useful form of complementary and alternative treatment.

Performing diaphragmatic breathing can be therapeutic, and with enough practice, can become a standard way of breathing. Start with 5 minutes and try to build up to 15 minutes.

Bubble of protection visualization

This exercise is great for when you feel vulnerable, intimidated, or just in need of protection in some way.

Shake out all the tension from your body and allow yourself to relax in whatever position you are in. Breathe naturally, in through your nose and out through your mouth.

Imagine a bubble of blue-white light all around you. You are safe inside. The bubble is charged with sparkling, protective energy. It moves with you and though it is soft on the inside, on the outside it is strong and is shielding you from whatever makes you anxious. It is keeping whatever worries you at a distance.

While you are inside the bubble, focus on your breathing. Breathe naturally, in through your nose and out through your mouth. Visualize the blue-white light flowing in and out of your pores as you inhale and exhale. The sparkling light is filling you with strength and energy.

Keep the bubble around you until the pressure has subsided and you feel comfortable enough to let it go, at least 10 minutes.

20

WRONG PERCEPTION BREATHING

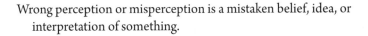

Wrong perception or misperception is a mistaken belief, idea, or interpretation of something.

Sit and close your eyes, breathing softly in and out, naturally in through your nose and out through your mouth.

Now, focus and see the roots of anger in your wrong perceptions or your unsupported assumptions and ignorance and breathe in.

Smile to your wrong perceptions and ignorance and breathe out.

Continue to seek out the wrong perceptions that have been troubling you and maintain this exercise for 10 minutes.

Wake-up call: awareness

Don't become the state of mind or the event you are experiencing—just let it pass through awareness without grabbing onto it. Non-judging awareness sees something as it is and lets it go. See it as process. The emotional stuff you take to be "you" is really not so personal.

21

WORK MEETING BREATHING

If you go to a lot of work meetings, make a card that says
BREATHE and put it somewhere where you can see it.

Whenever you feel agitated, bored, antsy, anxious, or feel your
mind wandering, look at the card. Stay in the present moment
and breathe. Take silent deep breaths, in through your nose and
out your mouth. The point is to concentrate on your breathing.

Wake–up call: balance

Think about how it is the hub or center of the wheel that
holds the rest of the wheel together and influences its
direction and speed in total balance. Try this affirmation:
I rest in tranquility and grace. I am calm, fulfilled, and
happy. I take refuge in my calm center and am balanced.
Repeat and believe.

22

Breathing for compassion

When you see an angry person suffering, do this exercise.

Breathe in and feel compassion for the angry person who suffers.

Breathe out, wishing the angry person to feel less suffering and let go of their angry feelings.

Repeat for 5 minutes.

Wake-up call: beauty

There is beauty in the ordinary. Finding beauty in the ordinary, and the ordinary in beauty, is Zen living in action. Meditation changes your response to stress and eliminates your response to yourself, because you begin to see things the way they really are—beautiful. You start to appreciate the beauty and wonder of the mundane.

23

LEANING PRANAYAMA

Pranayama is the formal practice for controlling the breath. It is a Sanskrit word meaning, "extension of the breath, the life force."

Stand and loosen your neck, arms, and hands and take deep breaths through your nose.

Close your eyes and set your feet about hip-width apart. Let your arms hang naturally.

Take a deep breath through your nose and lean to your right, exhaling through your nose.

At the end of the exhale, return to upright.

Now take in a new deep breath and lean to your left.

At the end of the exhale, return to upright.

Perform this up to 10 times for each side.

24

THIRD EYE BREATHING

Sit in a comfortable position and close your eyes.

Be with the breath. You can breathe normally or use ujjayi breath (drawing air in through both nostrils and breathing out with a slight constriction at the back of your throat, creating a whispering sound, like Darth Vader).

Put all your attention on the third eye area, right between your eyebrows.

You want to breathe in energy from the front of your forehead all the way to the back of the skull on the inhale and then reverse the process on the exhale.

As you do this, focus on the third eye and connect the sound of your breath to creating a physical vibration or feeling in your forehead. Doing this, you can create chi (the circulating life energy that is thought to be inherent in all things) and observe the very essence of breath, prana.

It is highly recommended to include third eye breathing whenever you can during your daily routines. You will notice how much more you are in the present moment.

25

Humming bee breath

Sit and close your eyes. Take a few focused, deeper-than-usual breaths. Allow your mind to focus and become calm. Bring your attention inward as you inhale through your nose. Make sure the inhalation is slow and long. Breathing in, contract your glottis (the opening between the vocal cords), making a snoring sound.

Once your lungs are filled, hold for as long as comfortable and then release through your nose.

As you exhale through your nose, make a soft humming sound in the mouth. This is a humming bee breath. Hum gently with your mouth closed but jaw relaxed. Continue the exhalation until the breath has completely exited your body.

Try this for 8–12 complete breaths. Let the sound vibrate in your head.

Then just sit quietly.

26

BE WITH THE BREATH

Take a moment. Feel yourself as the breath. Let go of watching
   your breath and instead enter the breath with all of your being.
   Let yourself be centered by the breath.

At first, be the swelling and receding, ebbing and flowing. Then
   become the stillness from which the breath arises. Become
   saturated with this stillness. Let yourself be the stillness that is
   your center.

Remain in stillness for 5 minutes or however long you
   feel comfortable.

Wake-up call: beginner's mind

For mindfulness, you need a beginner's mind:
non-judging, patient, trusting, non-striving, accepting,
and able to let go. In the beginner's mind, there are
many possibilities. In the beginner's mind, the mind is
willing to take in everything as if for the first time.
When you practice the beginner's mind, you encounter
each moment with fresh eyes and ears.

27

DEEP AND SLOW

Once a day, sit or lie down on the floor and stretch mindfully, staying in touch with your breathing.

Feel the breath moving in your body.

When you recognize a deep, slow breath, you can say DEEP as you breathe in and SLOW as you breathe out.

Do this for at least 5–10 minutes.

Wake-up call: belief

Suffering is caused by desire. Desire is wanting something you don't have, wishing something were some way it isn't, or being otherwise generally dissatisfied with the way things are. Desire is a belief that if things were better, you would be happier; life would be sweeter if only this were the case, if only that would happen, if only something were different than the way it is now. You create much "optional" suffering through the stories you tell yourself about what you believe will bring you happiness.

28

Kapalabhati technique

Kapalabhati consists of alternating short, explosive exhales and slightly longer, passive inhales. Exhales are generated by powerful contractions of the lower belly, which push air out of the lungs. Inhales are responses to the release of this contraction, which suck air back into the lungs.

Have a seat and close your eyes. Take in a very deep breath through your nose and when your lungs are completely full, quickly contract the belly and force the air out through your nose with a rapid, powerful push.

The abdomen moves like a bellows, drawing inward on exhalations. Repeat 3–10 times at about one exhale-inhale cycle every second or two.

At the end, take 2–3 deep breaths to bring your breathing back to normal.

As you become more adept at contracting/releasing your lower belly, you can increase your pace to about two exhale-inhale cycles every second and work up to 30–100 cycles.

29

Mind as gatekeeper

Make your mind a gatekeeper. A gatekeeper notices the fact that people are entering or leaving through the gate, but does not try to notice every little detail about each person.

Similarly, when you concentrate on sitting and breathing, you should not take into account the details of your experience. Simply notice the feeling of your inhaling and exhaling breath as it goes in and out right at the edges of your nostrils.

As you continue your practice, your mind and body become so light that you may feel as if you are floating. This is a sign of concentration.

Practice this for 5–10 minutes, or longer, if needed.

Wake-up call: calmness

By unifying the mind through calm practice, it becomes free, stable, unbound, and centered. In calm practice, every moment can be used to gain insight, and from that, calm arises. Learn the art of letting go and finding a calm center in the midst of everything. If your mind is calm and constant, you can keep yourself away from the noisy world even though you are in the midst of it. Your mind will be quiet and stable.

30

Arriving

Whenever you arrive at your destination, let yourself fully arrive. Rejoice.

Stand in front of your door and appreciate the moment of your arrival.

Pay attention. Take 3 deep breaths.

Explore the moment. Be awake. Be aware.

Notice the surroundings. Now open the door and step inside. Be mindful where you put your keys and other things.

Stay here for one minute.

Wake-up call: centering

If your mind is moving, you are not calm and centered. From a calm and peaceful center, you can respond instead of react. Wherever you are attached, like thinking about work while playing with your children or writing an email while your significant other is trying to talk to you, let go of that and come back to the center. The secret to living well is to "be" in the center of your "doing."

Deep release breathing

Sit in a comfortable position. Breathe in through the nose and then out through the mouth.

At the end of the exhale, pause, waiting patiently and consciously until the body initiates the next inhale. Every breath in is slow and calm through the nose.

At the top of the inhale, release air through the open mouth slowly and calmly, and then, with the mouth open and jaw relaxed, pause. Wait until the body chooses to inhale again.

During each pause, allow your body to deeply relax and let go.

You can also breathe into a specific body area in need of healing or relaxing and then consciously let all tension go with the exhale, relaxing further during the pause.

Deep-release breathing works best when done for 10 or more minutes.

32

EQUAL BREATHS

In this exercise, which can be done anytime and anywhere, simply count to 4 as you breathe in and count again to 4 as you breathe out.

Breathing in, feel happy. Breathing out, feel happy.

Even just a few relaxed breaths can make a big difference, but try to do this for 5–10 minutes for greater benefits.

Wake-up call: change

In life, all things change. Change is often different than you imagine and it can cause you to feel angry or defeated. Not only does the thing you want change, but your wants change, too. Can you think of any pain in your life that was not caused by change? Freedom and happiness are found in flexibility and the ease with which you deal with change. Whatever you cultivate during good times becomes your strength when things change.

33

On the hour mindful breathing

Set your watch or a clock to signal the beginning of every hour. When the alarm sounds, stop whatever you are doing and follow your breath with complete attention for 60 seconds.

Following the breath is paying attention to the quality of the breath at the point where you most strongly feel the sensation, usually at the nostrils.

If you are doing something that cannot be stopped, follow your breath as attentively as you can while engaging in the activity.

Practicing mindful breathing is finding an island within ourselves in which we can take refuge. It is an island of peace, confidence, solidity, love, and freedom.

Be an island within yourself. You don't have to look for it elsewhere. Mindful breathing helps you go back to that precious island within, so that you can experience the foundation of your being.

34

STOP AND SMELL THE ROSES

Look at the beauty of one flower. Stop and smell and smile.

Breathe in "one, two, three, four, five" while inhaling and "one, two, three, four, five" while exhaling.

Focusing on the flower while breath-counting occupies the mind so that the mind doesn't occupy you.

Stay with the flower for as long as you can.

Wake-up call: commitment

You need not look any farther ahead than to commit to taking one step. When you have taken one step, you can commit to taking another. During each step, commit yourself to gentleness and honesty. In this way, you demonstrate a commitment to non-harming and compassion. Make a commitment to staying awake and being mindful.

35

Walking meditation inside

Place the right fist, with thumb inside, on the chest and cover it
with the left palm while holding both palms at right angles.
Keep the arms in a straight line and the body erect, eyes resting
on a point about six feet in front of your feet.

Begin walking with the left foot and walk in such a way that
the foot sinks into the floor, first the heel and then the toes.
Count your inhalations and exhalations as you walk slowly
around the room.

Walk calmly and steadily, with poise and dignity.

Practice walking and breathing this way for at least 5 minutes
after each sitting period or do this as a separate exercise for
15–20 minutes.

Wake-up call: compassion

Once you understand that the basic nature of humanity
is compassionate rather than aggressive, your relationship
to the world changes immediately. It helps you relax,
trust, live at ease, and be happier. Compassion should
dominate our thoughts, words, and actions.

36

YIN BREATHING FOR KIDNEYS

Stand with your legs slightly bent in a squat, almost like sitting in a chair.

Place your palms or fingers on your lower back and breathe in and out slowly and calmly.

This releases the lower back muscles, lower part of the diaphragm, and cleanses and energizes the kidneys.

Yin breathing is like a slow ocean wave. Start first with your mouth open. Allow the breath to slow.

Count to 4 as you inhale, pause for 1 count, count to 4 as you exhale, and again pause for 1 count. This totals 10 counts. There is no need to overdo this.

The point is to remain aware of each breath. Stay with 6 breaths per minute cycle. When you can make the ocean sound continuously, try this with your mouth closed.

Yin breathing is done for mindfulness, and the longer you can do this, the more benefits you will receive.

37

ROLLDOWNS

Standing, let your head come forward until your chin is on your chest. Relax your jaw, opening your mouth and taking a few deep breaths in through your nose and out through your mouth.

Gradually roll down through each segment of your spine, knees bent, lengthening the spine.

After a few breaths, press down through your feet and curl back to standing. Make sure your knees are bent at the bottom of the movement and straight when you are totally upright.

Now turn your head to look over your right shoulder and slowly curl down to that side and then curl up, with the head, neck, and shoulders the last parts to come up.

Repeat to the left.

Do the whole series again, for a total of three cycles.

LENGTHENING THE BREATH

To work with fatigue, sit and settle into your everyday breath. After it has slowed down and smoothed out, pause after an exhalation. Rest in the stillness.

After a few seconds, you will feel a kind of ripple, which is the swell of your next inhalation. Don't take the inhalation immediately but instead allow it to gather for a few more seconds.

Continue lengthening your exhalation retentions for 10–15 breaths. Then begin to lengthen your inhalations gradually, too. This may work better than a cup of coffee to get you going again.

39

THREE–PART BREATHING

Sit comfortably, eyes closed. Put one palm on your belly and one on your chest, then inhale into the belly for 3 counts, then into your chest for 3 counts, then into your throat for 3 counts.

Three-part breathing is breathing all air out, then filling the belly, rib cage, and collarbone area before breathing out again.

Exhale from the belly for 3 counts, from the chest for 3 counts, and from your throat for 3 counts.

Watch carefully the turning point between 2 breaths.

Do this exercise 9 times.

40

FILLING AND EMPTYING THE LUNGS

Find a comfortable seated position. While breathing in through your nose, count, "one, one, one?" until the lungs are full of fresh air.

While breathing out, count, "two, two, two, two?" until the lungs are empty of fresh air.

Then while breathing in again count, "three, three, three, three, three?" until the lungs are full again and while breathing out count, "four, four, four, four?" until the lungs are empty of fresh air.

Count up to 10 and repeat as many times as necessary to keep the mind focused on the breath.

41

JUST SITTING

This exercise has two phases: just breathing and just sitting.
Once you are good at following your breath, you can practice
becoming your breath.

Merge yourself completely with the inhalations and exhalations.
It does not matter how you breathe, deep or short breaths. The
point is the breathing itself, not how you do the breathing. You
as a separate observer disappear and only your breath remains.
Your breath is breathing you.

Just sitting involves expanding to include all sense experiences—
seeing, smelling, hearing, thinking, touch. Instead of being
aware or mindful of these, you disappear and only the
experience remains.

Just sitting creates a calm and balanced state from which fresh
ideas are more likely to arise. Aim for 20 minutes of just sitting.

42

Calming anger

Sit and close your eyes. Breathe with your natural rhythm; no
need to change your breath.

Say, "Breathing in, I calm my anger." Then, "Breathing out, I take
care of my anger."

By doing this, you make your mind happy and at peace.

You may need time to calm your anger, so stay with this as long as
it takes to reach a point of equanimity.

Wake-up call: concentration

As the mind calms down, it naturally becomes more
concentrated. As your concentration deepens, you can
proceed to train the mind toward full concentration. The
joy you experience when you are practicing generosity
and morality gives rise to the happiness of concentration.
The Buddha called this purity of mind. When the mind is
steady and one-pointed, there is a quality of inner peace
and stillness that is much deeper and more fulfilling than the
happiness of sense pleasures. You enjoy sense pleasures,
like eating candy, but at a certain point you tire of them. By
contrast, the happiness that comes with concentration of
mind is refreshing. It energizes you. You never tire of it.

43

LETTING GO OF JUDGMENT

Sit quietly. Know you are breathing in. Know you are breathing out.

Be aware of a judgment thought within you. Maybe you are asking yourself why someone is dressed the way they are. Look deeply at it and its elements. Smile with compassion at the suffering these elements have caused.

Dwell in the present moment.

Breathe in and remember your good inner nature, your capacity for calm and compassion.

Breathe out and let go of judgment, without scolding yourself and creating a new judgment.

Sit for 20 minutes, using this time to let the breath help you let go of judgment.

Wake-up call: consciousness

Periodically survey your life and see what areas need more attention and consciousness. For example, try to practice mindful consumption. Vow to ingest only items that preserve peace, well-being, and joy in your body and in your consciousness.

44

Toning breath

Toning is the creation of extended vocal sounds on a single vowel in order to experience the sound and its effects in other parts of the body. Through toning you can immediately experience the effects of sound on your physical, mental, emotional, and spiritual well-being.

This toning breath exercise focuses on the principle sounds UU (grounding, calming, relaxing), EE (energizing, awakening), and AH (centering, expanding).

Lie down on your back with your knees bent. Relax and inhale through your nose.

Sound the syllables UU, EE, and AH on separate exhalations, taking a normal breath in and out between each syllable. Say UU, then breathe in and out. Say EE, then breathe in and out. Say AH, then breathe in and out.

Gradually increase the length of your exhalation sounds for 15–20 seconds. Do not strain; seek to have a smooth, open, easy feeling to your breathing.

Work up to 5–10 minutes on this exercise.

45

Smiling breath

Sit comfortably and close your eyes. As you inhale naturally, smile and sense your abdomen expanding with the spaciousness of your smiling breath. Your abdomen feels warm.

Exhale gently through the mouth while smiling. A spacious sensation spreads into your bones, organs, and tissues. You may also sense inner tensions and toxins going out with the exhalation.

You can come away from or dissolve a negative mind state, using smiling breath. Taoists say that when you smile, your organs release a honey-like secretion that nourishes the whole body.

Do smiling breath for 10–15 minutes.

Wake-up call: contact

The moment your mind is attentive to the contact between your body and the air, you are also in contact with your mind, just as it is. True mindfulness is an awareness that develops when your mind stays in contact with whatever you are doing.

46

STOP!

Stop! Every so often, just stop what you are doing and breathe, noticing the world all around you. Begin by saying "stop" and pausing the activity.

Open your senses to the environment.

Breathe slowly and deeply.

As you inhale, create space in your mind and environment.

As you exhale, imagine that time is expanding. Continue to do this, each time lengthening the out-breath.

Experience the present moment in complete stillness.

After a couple of minutes, resume what you were doing with a calmer mind.

47

INHALING ENERGY

Take a deep breath while sitting or standing.

Where do you feel your breathing?

What is the quality of your breathing?

Take another deep breath and imagine that you are pulling your energy back into your body. You will immediately feel more grounded, centered, powerful.

This is a very quick, but helpful practice.

Wake-up call: contentment

Contentment comes from neither doing nor having, but from being. Suffering is caused by craving and aversion. You will suffer if you expect other people to conform to your expectations, if you want others to like you, if you do not get something you want, etc. Even getting what you want does not guarantee contentment and happiness. Rather than constantly struggling to get what you want, try to modify your wanting. Wanting deprives you of contentment and happiness.

48

BREATHING FOR MIND AWARENESS

Sit with your eyes closed. Breathe naturally.

Say, "Breathing in, I am aware of my mind. Breathing out, I am aware of my mind."

This means that as soon as a mental formation or thought arises, you should breathe in and out and identify the mental formation.

To identify a mental formation with the help of conscious breathing means to recognize, embrace, and become one with that mental formation. You are not clinging to it or pushing it away. You are learning to see something that enters your mind and simply identifying it. This cultivates acceptance and mindfulness.

Practice this for at least 10 minutes.

Wake-up call: contribution

What makes you happy most likely will also be a worthwhile contribution to the world. What contribution have you made to the world that gives your heart the greatest satisfaction? Can you be of further service? Should you start now?

49

Dying with each exhalation

The fear of dying can be mitigated by meditating upon death. Do this by dying a little with each exhalation. Thinking about death is wasting the present moment, so an exercise that increases your awareness of the present moment makes you feel more alive.

With each exhalation, die into the present moment.

Whatever sensations you may feel, let go of them. Let go of any attempts to control the mind.

Breath by breath, forgive others. Forgive those from the past as well as those who are still around you. Forgive yourself.

Accept others for who they are. Accept yourself totally. Let go and relish the freedom of desirelessness.

Each moment is the only moment you truly have.

This important exercise should be practiced for 15 minutes.

50

PUSH THE MOUNTAIN

Stand with arms at your sides, eyes closed. Take a deep breath into your nose and hold it in your abdomen to a count of 10. Then release through your nose.

On the second breath, breathe in slowly and deeply through your nose, taking a step forward with your left leg.

Inhaling, raise your hands, bending at the elbows so your palms are facing away at chest level. Hold this breath for a count of 10.

As you exhale, tighten the muscles of your shoulders, back, arms, and hands. Push forward with your open palms, visualizing a mountain in front of you moving with the power of your push. Hold for a 10 count.

Inhale and step forward with your right leg and bring your palms back to your chest for a count of ten.

When it is time to exhale, push the mountain again.

Do this exercise up to 10 times.

51

BREATHING ON THE BEACH

Visualize yourself on a beach.

On each inhale, feel the warmth of the sun and the touch of the breeze. Let your breathing coincide with the rhythm of the waves.

Feel tension release from your body during each exhale.

If you use ujjayi breath (lightly constricting the back of the throat to create a whispering sound as you breathe), this will tighten your stomach muscles, too, and help push out leftover air from your lungs. You can increase your exhalation using these methods, too: blowing through a musical instrument, blowing bubbles, singing a song, or chanting.

Enjoy this breath of renewal for 10–20 minutes.

Wake-up call: cooking

Happy cooks make happy food. To cook is not just to prepare food—it is an expression. Allow plenty of time to prepare your meal. Work on it with nothing in your mind and without expecting anything. Just cook!

52

Cleansing breath

Breathing in through the nose, feel the air coming in through the soles of your feet. Breathe in as if you have to pull the air up through your feet and body, until you blow it out through your open mouth.

Continue for several breaths, drawing the air in through your feet and up through your body, then blowing it out, slowly and calmly.

Imagine you are sweeping up all the energy in your system with the inhale and that as it emerges from your body on the exhale, this energy bursts out into sparks.

Continue this for several minutes.

Wake-up call: courage

Relinquishment is learning to keep letting go, which takes courage. Have the courage to let a thought slip by and not chase after it. If someone makes a negative comment to you, let it go. It is only by a courageous letting go that the heart becomes free.

53

Humming

Sit in a relaxed position with eyes closed and lips together.

Start humming, loudly enough that you start to create a vibration throughout your body. Breathe in and out through your nose. You can visualize a hollow tube or an empty vessel, filled only with the vibrations of the humming.

A point will come when the humming continues by itself and you become the listener. You can alter the pitch or move your body smoothly and slowly if you feel it.

The second stage is divided into two 7½ minute sections. For the first half, move the hands, palms up, in an outward circular motion. Starting at the navel, both hands move forward and then divide to make two large circles mirroring each other left and right. The movement should be slow enough that at times there will appear to be no movement at all. Feel that you are giving energy outward to the universe.

After 7½ minutes, turn the hands palms down and start moving them in the opposite direction. Now the hands will come together toward the navel and divide outward to the sides of the body. Feel that you are taking energy in.

Then sit absolutely quiet and still for a couple minutes, breathing in and out naturally, before returning to your day.

54

BREATHING WITH WATER

Get in a comfortable position, either sitting or standing, and relax. Fill your mouth with water and keep it there for 5 minutes. Remember to breathe in and out of your nose.

If you breathe in mindfully and smile lightly, you relax the hundreds of muscles in your face.

The combination of having water in your mouth, breathing mindfully, and smiling will create a pleasant feeling. It is amazing how much concentration you will feel after doing this.

Wake-up call: creativity

Put aside judgment, preconceived notions, fears, and what is standing between you and creativity. Creativity is a product of a clear, unobstructed mind. Creative problem-solving is best accomplished when the mind is open to all possible solutions. One effective way to achieve a creative solution quickly is by doing controlled breathing exercises.

FULL–BODY BREATH

Stand and as you inhale through your nose, slowly rise up on your toes and simultaneously raise your arms up in front of you and over your head, palms facing forward.

As you exhale, slowly lower your arms and feet to the starting position.

Do this for a few minutes, sending your full-body energy connecting heaven and earth. You will instantly experience a positive feeling throughout your body.

Wake-up call: curiosity

Curiosity is not one of the classic virtues, but it's a sign of mental and imaginative engagement with life, and a cornerstone of creativity. Stay curious and you'll never have time to be bored.

56

WAKING UP

Before you get out of bed each morning, take five minutes to lie
very still.

Listen, see, smell, breathe.

Do not judge; just observe and breathe mindfully.

See if you can become aware of a space opening inside your
breath. As this space opens, see what happens to your
awareness of the sounds in your surroundings.

Allow your breathing to lead you into awareness of the day you
are entering.

57

MEDITATION MINUTE

Make a determination to meditate for one minute of every hour throughout the day.

Stop whatever you are doing and follow the breath with full attention for 60 seconds. Breathe in and out normally. Relax and concentrate for the full 60 seconds.

Healing begins with a breath.

Wake-up call: desirelessness

Relinquishment of craving, clinging, and attachment leads to desirelessness and nirvana starts to seep in. Relinquishing attachment, little by little, does ultimately pay off. Do a meditation of letting go a little with each exhalation. Let go into the present moment. Whatever sensations you may feel, let go of them. Let go of any attempts to control the mind. Breath by breath, forgive others. Forgive those from the past as well as those who are still around you. Forgive yourself. Accept others for what they are. Accept yourself totally. Let go and let be. Fly free. Soar in the freedom of desirelessness.

58

Eating mindfully

If you eat with others who are not eating mindfully, you can still stop every once in a while and look around, breathe, and smile. Remember: most of the time, you are probably more hungry for breath than you are for food.

Train yourself to breathe in and out, focusing on stopping or pausing.

Concentrate on breathing in for 5 seconds and then breathing out for 5 seconds between bites of food. Breathing in and out during eating trains yourself to eat more mindfully while filling your body with oxygen. It makes the entire eating process much more enjoyable, satisfying, and peaceful.

Be grateful for the elements of the meal and for where they came from. Be grateful you have food and are sharing it with others.

Wake-up call: dignity

Choose to speak in a way that fosters dignity, respect, and simplicity. When you simplify your communications by eliminating the irrelevant, you infuse what you do communicate with greater importance, dignity, and intention. Before you speak, remind yourself to express dignity and respect.

59

DEEP RELAXATION BEFORE SLEEP

Lying down in bed in deep relaxation mediation, as you breathe in and out, become aware of your whole body letting go. Relax more with each natural breath in and out.

Feel all the areas of your body that are touching the bed you are lying on.

With each out-breath, feel yourself sink deeper and deeper into the surface, letting go of tension and worries, not holding on to anything.

Send your love and compassion to your whole body. Feel gratitude for all the cells in your body. The oxygen from each in breath is nourishing them.

Concentrate on quieting the breath, focusing on its rhythm. You will develop a natural, relaxing rhythm that will follow you to sleep.

Wake-up call: diligence

Diligence helps foster the conditions of happiness. Persistence and diligence almost always pay off. Artists know that diligence counts as much, if not more, as inspiration. As Samuel Johnson said, "What we hope ever to do with ease, we must learn first to do with diligence."

60

CIRCULATING ENERGY BREATH

Sit and close your eyes. Breathe slowly in and out through the nose.

As you breathe in, feel you are drawing air in through your left hand and up your arm to your neck.

Breathing out, allow the energy to flow down your right arm and out your right hand.

Continue this for several breaths, then reverse the flow from right to left.

Now switch to your legs, inhaling up the left leg to the base of your spine and exhaling down your right leg for several breaths.

Then reverse to go up the right leg and down the left leg.

Finally, start the breath at the base of the spine, inhaling the energy up to the top of your head and then exhaling it across your face, throat, chest, belly, and to the base of the spine. This should feel like a waterfall on the exhale.

Do this for three cycles if possible.

61

Diaphragmatic breathing

Lie down with the fingers of your hands over the base of your rib cage. Relax your body. Press to create a little resistance.

Begin to direct and expand your breath into the ribs, expanding the ribs out to the sides against the pressure of your hands.

With each breath, the fingers move away and then come together like an accordion. Provide firm resistance with your hands.

Rest after 10 cycles, then do another two sets of 10 cycles.

(You can also make a 1- to 10-pound sand or rice or bean bag to rest on your chest, which is very useful for strengthening the diaphragm.)

Wake-up call: discipline

When you are tempted to buy another pretty sweater when your closet is full of them, discipline the mind. Ignore the thought, divert the mind, replace the greedy thought with a generous one, reflect mindfully on the impermanent nature of sweaters. If the mind is still whining and crying, you may need to get harsh with yourself. Give yourself an ultimatum to do something useful. The mind can be trained to let go.

62

Running through a forest

Imagine you are running through a dark forest. It is hard to see anything, but you can feel the dirt path under your feet and the thick forest around you. Then pause and take some deep breaths. Begin running in your mind again.

When you do this, envision running to a clearing up ahead. The forest opens up and there is bright daylight surrounding your body.

You reach the clearing and rest there momentarily. Again, pause for 30 seconds and take some deep, even breaths.

Then you see a path leading out of the clearing into the forest and you follow this path until you emerge back into sunlight. Then you see a path leading out of the clearing back into the dark forest. You take the path. Then pause for 30 seconds and take deep, even breaths.

Do this exercise for 10 minutes, going into the dark forest and then finding the clearing that makes everything bright.

63

SMILING AT BODY PARTS

Sit with the eyes closed, and know you are breathing in. Know you are breathing out. This awareness will help you concentrate.

Be aware of the hair on top of your head. Smile to the hair on your head. Breathe naturally.

Be aware of the soles of your feet. Smile to the soles of your feet.

Dwell in the present moment. Be aware this is the only moment when you are alive.

Stay here for 10–20 minutes, smiling at all your body parts.

As Thích Nhất Hạnh says, sometimes your joy is the source of your smile, but sometimes your smile is the source of your joy.

Wake-up call: effort

Happiness does not come automatically. It is not a gift that good fortune bestows upon us and a reversal of fortune takes back. It depends on us alone. One does not become happy overnight, but with patient labor, day after day. Happiness is constructed, and that requires effort and time. In order to become happy, you have to learn how to change yourself.

64

Tibetan rebalancing breath

Sit with your hands on your knees and close your eyes gently. Feel your body relax.

Inhaling through your nose, sweep your left arm up in an arc, then bend your elbow at the peak and close the left nostril with the left thumb.

Smoothly exhale through your right nostril. At the end of the exhale, return to the starting position.

Inhaling through your nose, sweep your right arm up in an arc, then bend your elbow at the peak and close the right nostril with the right thumb.

Smoothly exhale through your left nostril. At the end of the exhale, return to the starting position, sitting with your hands on your knees and your eyes closed.

Repeat the movement on the right side, sweeping your right arm up.

Do this 6 times on each side.

65

BALLOON BREATHING

Sitting or standing, sense the entire space bounded by your navel, your pubic bone, and your lower back.

As you inhale, visualize and sense that a balloon is inflating in your belly. As you inhale, feel the balloon expanding forward, backward, and to the sides. As you breathe in, the balloon expands and gets bigger.

As you breathe out, the balloon contracts and you have the sensation that the air is squeezed slowly back up through and out your nose.

While you do this exercise, sense the downward and upward movement of the diaphragm as you inhale and exhale. It moves up with each inhalation and down with each exhalation.

You will feel warmth in your abdomen, a kind of energy. Remain with this exercise for 5–20 minutes.

66

RELAXING THE EYES

Find a quiet and dimly lit place to do this exercise. Relax your eyes.

Breathing quietly, gently rotate your eyes in each direction, then stop and let your eyes relax into their sockets. Repeat this several times.

By relaxing your eyes, you can relax your whole body and thus free your energy.

Wake-up call: empathy

Appreciating another's achievement is an important aspect of empathy. Take every opportunity to celebrate success with friends and family. A surprise present needs no better pretext. Feeling another person's joy is a sure sign of a magnanimous spirit, and one that brings its own reward.

67

Mindful commuting

When you first sit down in the car, bus, or train, take 3 breaths. Be mindful and aware of the experience. Concentrate on the breath.

During the commute, notice the environment. Be aware of the weather, the other cars, the other people. Be part of the journey.

Sit calmly, letting each breath clear your mind and open your heart. When you arrive at your destination, take another moment to sit calmly, letting each breath clear your mind and open your heart.

Be here now. You are prepared to begin your next task.

Breathing will help you free yourself. It will free you from the grasp of your little mind.

Wake-up call: energy

Energy storms come and go in the mind, stirring up restlessness. Acknowledge this and breathe long, slow, deliberate breaths. Relaxed breathing calms the body and settles the mind. Energy levels change in the mind just as they do in the body. Acknowledge your energy state, whatever it is. Keep your eyes open. Try to aim the mind precisely by noting the beginning and ending of each breath.

ACTIVITIES WITH MINDFUL BREATH

Incorporate breathing into activities by first using slow, rhythmic body movement. Whether you are reading, exercising, or watching television, incorporating your breathing into these activities will cultivate your awareness.

As your breathing slows to match the activity, you will find your mind entering a state of tranquility. You will be relaxed and focused at the same time. You will be in the zone while completing your activity.

It only takes one conscious breath to be in touch with ourselves and the world around us. With each additional conscious breath, you will continue to be in touch with yourself and the world around you, one breath at a time.

Wake-up call: equanimity

A steady investigation can bring equanimity to whatever is happening. Acknowledge to yourself that all created things arise and pass away. Acknowledge that all beings are heirs to their own karma. Accepting this allows you to find balance and equanimity and peace. Say, "May I accept things as they are. May I remain undisturbed by changing events."

69

Rhythmic breathing

Rhythmic breathing will give you energy, help you relax, and enhance concentration.

Sit comfortably with your eyes closed. Breathe in through the nose for a slow count of 8, hold for 4 counts, breathe out through the nose for a slow count of 8, and then pause for 4 counts.

Some people are more comfortable practicing rhythmic breathing with a lower count, which is fine. So, alternatively: inhale for 4 counts, hold for 2 counts, exhale for 4 counts, pause for 2 counts.

Continue for 10 minutes, if possible.

Wake-up call: exercise

Be mindful of your need for exercise and honor it. Mindful exercise means keeping body and mind involved together in an exercise activity—no books, telephone, headphones, etc. Bringing the mindfulness techniques you are already working with to your physical exercise can put you in the zone faster and keep you there longer.

70

LION BREATH

Sit or kneel with the legs crossed and inhale deeply through both nostrils to the count of four.

While holding in the breath, curl your tongue backward until it hits the roof of your mouth.

Then simultaneously open your mouth wide and stretch your tongue out, curling its tip down toward the chin. Open your eyes wide, contract the muscles at the front of your throat, and exhale the breath slowly out through your mouth with a distinct HA sound, a human "roar." The breath should pass over the back of the throat.

You can roar 2–3 times. Then change the cross of the legs and repeat for 2–3 times.

71

CALMING WALK

Take a walk on the calm side. If you are feeling foggy, walk to clear your head. Breathe normally with no thought about the breathing process. The breathing exercise will come in at the end of your walk.

Imagine clouds in your mind dissipating. See the clouds floating away and blue sky replacing them.

At the end of your walk, gently shake your head and take 3 deep breaths. Feel the calm that is now with you.

Wake-up call: faith

Faith can determine destiny. Your faith in the practices of mindfulness, in the unerring rightness of what this moment offers you, will help you walk through many doors that otherwise might be closed to you. Faith means trusting the unfolding process of your life. It is a willingness to let go of fears and attachments and open yourself to the unknown in each new moment. You have to believe inner peace is possible, that you are already perfect, that you don't need to add anything to yourself.

72

Field of vision

Breathe deeply with your eyes closed, in and out. Let the thoughts, feelings, and preoccupations you have disperse. Release them with each breath.

Then open your eyes and look at everything and everyone in your field of vision as though for the last time. Consider the beauty and preciousness of this moment, which is the only one you have. You are in that moment. Reflect on the recognition that every moment is like this one.

Breathe into the present moment and stay here as long as you can, 5–20 minutes.

At the end of the meditation, retain the insights you have gained as you continue through your day.

Wake-up call: fearlessness

Our two most fundamental emotions are love and fear, which in some sense are opposites of each other. Fear is often the thing that prevents our capacity for love from finding its true fulfillment. Love, on the other hand, can vaporize fear into non-existence. Love makes us move toward someone; fear makes us shrink away. Find love and be fearless. Have the fearless attitude of a hero and the loving heart of a child.

73

ELONGATING THE BREATH

For 5–10 minutes, sit in a comfortable position. Breathe smoothly in your habitual breathing pattern. When you first begin to observe your breath, you will be observing your *habitual* breath. This exercise will help you recognize any inhibitions and restrictions that define your habitual breath.

Then slightly elongate your inhalations and exhalations but focus on smoothness and ease.

It is important to just slightly elongate the breath, so you move from habitual breath to natural breath. Moving into your natural breath is like lying on the earth and calmly watching the clouds go by. Breathing naturally will help you feel refreshed, balanced, and content.

This is an exercise to practice many times, to move toward more natural breathing. Learning natural breathing is an ongoing practice. The more you practice, the more you'll move toward natural balance and a natural state of contentment.

74

Inner smile

Whenever you are just sitting, relax your lower jaw and open your mouth slightly. Try to make your breath very shallow and relax your whole body. This is not deep breathing through your diaphragm, but rather quick and shallow breathing through your throat.

Start feeling a smile in your inner being, like in your belly. Let this smile spread from inside to your whole body. You are one big smile now.

You can use this any time. You can practice the inner smile in any situation—while sitting, lying down, standing, driving, or working. Breathing consciously and smiling will bring more awareness and concentration to whatever you are doing.

Wake-up call: flexibility

Freedom and happiness are found in flexibility and the ease with which you deal with change. Meditation and breathing exercises help you learn to put distance between yourself and your thoughts. With practice, your mind becomes flexible and pliable and you have more clarity about your direction in life. Flexible, adaptable species survive and thrive while those that are inflexible become extinct.

Hara (Abdominal) Breathing

Abdominal breathing—especially when it is slow, deep, and long—combined with certain mindfulness practices directed to specific energy centers, can help you receive the energies of the earth, nature, and the heavens. In natural breathing, when you breathe in, a respiratory wave starts deep in the abdominal cavity and flows up to the head. When you breathe out, the wave moves from head to feet.

To sense your power center (*hara*), lie in relaxation pose. Hara breathing can be done standing, sitting, or lying down. The *hara* is located two inches below the navel. It's the physical and spiritual center of the body.

Cover the navel with your hands. Breathe gently, in through the nose, filling the abdomen with air, and focus on your navel.

On the exhale through your mouth, contract the muscles of your abdomen. Tighten the abdomen as much as you can.

Continue until you feel your breath being drawn from deep within your *hara*. When you breathe from your navel, you will feel the abdomen expand and contract.

Take a deep breath and feel the diaphragm muscle move downward on inhalation and upward on exhalation. Do this exercise anytime, for as long as you can, but at least 5–10 minutes.

76

BREATH PAUSES

Sit or lie in a comfortable position. You can use a chair, gomden, mat, or bed. The important thing is to be comfortable.

Follow your breathing. Notice the two pauses in your breathing cycle: one after inhalation and one after exhalation.

Pay particular attention to the pause after exhalation. This pause is an important entranceway into the healing spaciousness of your own self.

Do this for 10 minutes.

Wake-up call: flow

A life filled with complex flow activities is more worth living than one spent consuming passive entertainment. Breathing exercises help you cultivate the conscious intention to transcend yourself and to enter into the flow of consciousness. If you are interested in something, you will focus on it, and if you focus attention on anything, it is likely that you will become interested in it. Many of the things you find interesting are not so by nature, but because you took the trouble of paying attention to them.

77

POWER BREATH

Sit and inhale powerfully through your nose while lifting your arms straight over your shoulders.

Powerfully exhale through your nose while bringing your hands back next to your shoulders.

Repeat this as quickly and intensely as you can for 60 seconds.

The more powerfully and rapidly you do each breath, the more effect you will feel.

Take one last deep breath and hold it for as long as you can. When you release this breath, you will feel the new energy that is in your mind and body.

78

KRAMA BREATHING

Krama means "step" or "stage" and this breathing method can enhance your sense of self by peacefully and gradually filling your body with fresh life force.

Sit and focus on your tailbone, with your spine as straight as possible, like a string is pulling you up.

You are going to divide your breath into 3 parts. Inhale the first third of the breath from your tailbone to the top of your pelvis, then hold.

In the second phase, feel your breath moving from the top of your pelvis to the space behind your heart and hold lightly.

On the third part of the inhalation, sense your breath moving from your heart to the crown of your head and hold again.

Exhale, releasing the breath in a wave from the crown of your head to your tailbone.

Repeat 3 times. With each full breath, feel the fresh life force filling your body.

79

LOOK AT YOU

Imagine yourself in front of you and become aware of your own stress, suffering, and dissatisfaction. Feel compassion for yourself.

On the inhale, breathe in suffering and take it into your heart's sphere of light.

Breathe out soothing, compassionate energy. Feel the energy pass through your entire body.

Complete this exercise for the stress and the dissatisfaction in your life. Substitute stress and dissatisfaction with compassion each time you do the exercise.

Do this compassion exercise for yourself for 10–20 minutes.

80

WHOLE-BODY BREATHING

In whatever position is comfortable, try to sense your whole body involved in breathing. Find a position that is comfortable for you. When you are in this position, try to sense your whole body involved in the act of breathing—not just your diaphragm or throat, but your entire body.

As you inhale, you may feel a sensation in your feet bubbling up through the tissues and organs, moving to the top of your head. Relish this feeling. This is your whole body breathing.

As you exhale, you may sense the inner energy of the breath spreading downward toward your feet. Feel the energy travel from the top of your head all the way down to your feet.

Become totally aware of this breath. Observe any areas where the breath does not move or penetrate. With each inhalation and exhalation, let the breath flow through those areas. Work for at least 10 minutes this way.

TRANSFORMING IRRITATION

Everyone from time to time feels irritated. When you do feel irritated, see that it is not an enemy. Do not let it take control of your life.

Breathe in through your nose and out through your mouth with awareness. With every breath, become more aware of the breath.

You do not need to wipe out the irritation, but rather treat it with compassion as if holding a baby in your arms.

This breathing exercise brings awareness and your irritation is gradually transformed.
We have to stop, pay attention, breathe, and transform anger into compassion.

Do this exercise for at least 5 minutes.

82

Triangle breathing

Visualize a triangle in your mind.

Inhale through the nose for a count of 4.

Hold the air in your lungs for a count of 4.

Exhale through the nose for a count of 4.

Move from point to point in this triangle for 3–4 minutes.

Visualize a triangle and move point to point during this. Continue for 3–4 minutes.

Wake-up call: forgiveness

Forgiveness of yourself is at the heart of all happiness, the ground for any healing. If there are ways you have harmed yourself or not loved yourself or not lived up to your own expectations, this is the time to let go of the unkindness you feel toward yourself. Say, "for all of the ways I have harmed or hurt myself, knowingly or unknowingly, I offer myself forgiveness." You can do this as part of your daily meditation and let your intention to forgive yourself work over time. Imagine 7 billion souls, showing courage, compassion, or forgiveness in countless ways. Make forgiveness a practice.

83

MINDFUL EXERCISING

The next time you exercise, make a point of following your breathing as much as you can.

Be mindful of your body as you move, as well as your breath. Whether running, walking, or any other kind of exercise, concentrate on your breath. Your breathing may become louder to you as you become more mindful of it.

If you are taken away from concentrating on your breathing, note what took you away and then quickly return to your experience. It does not matter how many times you have to do this. The important thing is to get back to following your breathing.

Try to do this mindful breathing for at least 10 minutes, but ideally for the length of your exercise program.

Wake-up call: freedom

True freedom is realizing that there is nothing to hold onto that can offer lasting satisfaction, which shows us there is nowhere to go and nothing to have and nothing to be. Each moment of non-wanting is a moment of freedom. Mindfulness allows non-wanting. When there is clear attention, when there is just watching, there is not wanting and freedom takes its place.

84

ATTENTION TO THE BREATH'S SUBTLE CHANGES

Sit comfortably, noticing that even in its regularity the breath goes through subtle changes. It can increase or decrease in rate and depth.

The sensations that accompany the in-breath are somewhat different from the sensations that accompany the out-breath.

As you relax and let the breath happen all by itself, you will be able to sharpen your attention by noticing how interesting and complex the simple act of breathing is. It is our life force, yet, normally, we pay absolutely no attention to it. During exercise, we are changing that. We are noticing the subtle changes and sensations that accompany the act of breathing.

Rest in the breath's regularity and notice its constant, subtle changes for 5–10 minutes or more.

BREATHING WITH FEELINGS

Know you are breathing in. Know you are breathing out.

Be aware of a pleasant feeling arising. Hold this feeling as though it was your most precious child. Smile with joy at your happiness.

Then be aware of an unpleasant feeling arising. Be aware that you dislike this feeling. Hold this feeling as though it was your most precious child. Smile with compassion at your suffering.

Be aware of either feeling arising and passing away. Accept this.

Dwell in the present moment for 5–10 minutes or more.

Wake-up call: friendship

Think about what friendship means to you and what you value most in a friend. Think about what you would like to offer to others as a friend. Good friends are a great resource for happiness and freedom. Our society is built on communication: our culture, our systems, our friendships, our love—the whole world around us. But, just like forgiveness, you first have to be a friend to yourself before you can truly be a friend to others.

Paragraph breath breaks

While reading, do mini-breathing meditations, like for five seconds at the end of a page or at the end of a chapter. This will keep you from falling asleep while reading or having to reread paragraphs because you were not concentrating on the words. It is a very simple breathing exercise and can be done throughout your reading.

Pause and take a conscious breath.

Then move on.

Also, try stopping every half hour. Stop reading and close your eyes for a minute or so and bring your attention back to your breath.

As you get used to the idea of this, you may sometimes slip into breath meditation and decide to stop reading for a while.

87

LAUGHING

Sit down, relax. Breathe and smile. Be happy and peaceful.

Practice laughing and smiling yoga meditation. Smile. Smile
even more. Smile as if you were enlightened. Grin. Be silly.
Relax your mind. Change the smile into laughter. Increase the
laughter. Be happy. See how good it feels to laugh and be happy.

See how that feels. Imagine what it looks like.

Do this for as much time as you feel comfortable.

88

HA BREATH

The HA breath is a great, quick exercise to do before meals.

Stand up. Inhale through the nose, tilt your head back, pause.

Then exhale HA! through the mouth.

Do these 10 quick breaths before each meal.

Wake-up call: generosity

If you consistently cultivate generosity to all, you'll make lots of friends, many will love you, and you'll feel relaxed and peaceful. Generosity is giving, yielding, unconditional love, an outstretched hand, open mind, open heart. Every act of generosity slowly weakens the factor of greed. Just remember that generosity is not about giving "things" so that you are thanked and appreciated. It is done selflessly and with no expectations of a return or thanks. For example, practicing generosity in human relationships means trusting another person and allowing him or her to enjoy space and freedom and dignity.

89

COOLING BREATH

Try this twice a day, or as needed during stressful times. It is also
called Sitali Pranayama, which translates to cooling breath.

Sit comfortably in a chair or on the floor, shoulders relaxed,
spine erect.

Observe your breath with eyes closed. Slightly lower the chin.
Then curl your tongue and extend it through your lips. Bring
air in through this central passageway.

As you inhale gently, slowly lift your chin toward the ceiling,
lifting only as far as the neck is comfortable.

At the end of the inhale, bring your tongue in and close your lips.
Hold for as long as comfortable.

Then exhale gently through your nose as you lower your chin back
to a neutral position.

It is like drinking a glass of cool lemonade on a hot day and feeling
your body becoming cool inside. When you breathe in, the air
enters your body and calms all the cells of your body.

Experience light emptiness and then perform the breath again, for
8–12 cycles.

ENERGY BALL

Sit or stand and watch your breath for several minutes. Make sure there is a balanced rhythm to your breathing.

Then put your hands over your abdomen and feel the energy ball behind your navel expanding as you inhale and contracting as you exhale.

Let the energy ball spread into your solar plexus, just below your sternum.

As you exhale, feel the solar plexus and navel areas contracting. Your breath will slow.

Do this for several minutes.

Wake-up call: goals

Try less and "be" more. Back off from striving for goals and instead start focusing carefully on seeing and accepting things as they are, moment by moment. Do not struggle to achieve; drop the fear of failure. Relax and be at ease. Things should not bother you—just let them happen. Get the tight, grasping, goal-oriented mind to relax. Your goal is not external and distant. The path is the goal.

RESTING IN THE PAUSE

Sit or stand comfortably, breathing in and out slowly and deeply.
Allow your attention to be "captured" by the pause between the
rising and falling of the breath.

Feel yourself recline into that pause as if lying back into the arms
of someone you trust with your life.

Notice that in the pause there is no thought, no sensation—
only stillness.

This is the root of the breath. It is spacious and expansive. Allow
yourself to become this stillness, this expanse. The stillness has
always been present within you, waiting to be discovered.

Make this practice a habit by doing it regularly, at least 5 minutes
per session.

92

COMMERCIAL MUTE

During television commercials, hit mute and take some mindful breaths. Nothing complicated, just some mindful breaths for a minute or two. Concentrate on each breath. Relax your body and follow the natural rhythm that occurs from this mindful breathing. When the commercial is over, go back to enjoying your show.

Wake-up call: gratitude

Happiness cannot be traveled to, owned, earned, worn, or consumed, but it can be appreciated. Happiness is the spiritual experience of living every minute with love, grace, and gratitude. Have a sense of gratitude for everything—even difficult emotions, because of their potential to wake you up.

93

BASIC LISTENING MEDITATION

Sit comfortably, whatever that is for you. Let your eyes close
gently. Invite your body to relax and release into the ground or
cushion. Let go and accept the non-doing of meditation.

Become sensitive to and listen to your breath. Breathe through
your nose. Feel the air as it goes in and out of the nostrils. Feel
the rising and falling of the chest and abdomen. Allow your
attention to settle into ambient sound.

Follow the breath and listen. Subtly note the nuances of the
sounds for 20 minutes.

As you gently open your eyes, try to carry the momentum of your
mindfulness into whatever your next activity may be.

94

Breath pumping

Lie on the floor, knees slightly bent. Relax with a few deep belly breaths.

Inhale through your nose until your belly is round like a balloon. Lock in that breath.

While holding your breath, flatten your back and belly, forcing the balloon of air upward in your chest, not letting air out.

Then flatten your chest, pushing the air back to the belly while arching your back. Continue this pumping movement until you need to take a breath. When you need to exhale, do so out of your mouth.

Do this exercise for 10 rounds.

WASHING BY HAND

When washing clothes or dishes by hand, scrub the items in a relaxed way. Breathe naturally and steadily.

Pay attention to every movement, to the soap and water. More than 90 percent of the time, your body feels air. Now you are feeling and sensing water. Become totally aware of the sensations of touching water.

Maintain a half-smile and follow your breath. If your mind wanders, come back by maintaining a half-smile and following your breath. This will bring you back.

When you have finished, you should feel as clean as your clothes or dishes.

Knitted body

Imagine that your skin is like a knitted bodysuit that covers all of you, something comfortable that your grandmother or aunt made for you.

As you inhale through your nose, feel how the knitted strands stretch and spread apart, creating spaces between them all over your body.

As you exhale, feel how the strands retract and the fibers become more dense and opaque.

Enjoy the whole feeling of the body swelling and retracting, filling and emptying. Do this exercise for 20 minutes.

97

DEEP EXHALES

Deliberately take in a very deep breath and as soon as your lungs are full, immediately exhale through your mouth.

Do this for 3–4 cycles.

Then, after a deep inhale, as soon as your lungs are full, hold your breath for 2 seconds, then exhale through your mouth.

Do this, too, for 3–4 cycles.

Wake-up call: harmony

To create peace in the world, you must be unruffled within and in harmony with yourself and others. Walk in stillness, act and work in harmony with the middle way. The serenity that emanates from you will create peace and all things will flourish. Tranquility is achieved when you are in harmony with all beings and all situations, knowing that everything is precisely the way it is meant to be.

BREATHING WITH AWARENESS

Sometimes simply being conscious of breathing in and breathing out can move you into a place of greater peace, health, and awareness. Thích Nhất Hạnh teaches that mindful breathing can bring healing and transformation to your mind and body. Read through these affirmations as you breathe, allowing the words to become part of the rhythm of your breath. Feel free to re-read any of these affirmations multiple times as you breathe, until the words sink in and feel real.

1. Breathing in deeply, I am aware that I'm breathing in deeply. Breathing out slowly, I am aware that I'm breathing out slowly.
2. Breathing in deeply, I feel my body, from my toes through the top of my head. Breathing out slowly, I feel my body, from the top of my head down through my toes.
3. Breathing in deeply, I feel peace moving up through the soles of my feet and out through the top of my head. Breathing out slowly, I feel peace washing through my head and down through my toes.
4. Breathing in deeply, I feel joy moving through every cell of my body. Breathing out slowly, I feel joy moving through every cell of my body.
5. Breathing in deeply, I feel joy and peace meeting in my heart center. Breathing out slowly, I feel joy and peace flowing out through my fingertips.
6. Breathing in deeply, I feel my mind clear and sharp. Breathing out slowly, I feel my mind clear and sharp.
7. Breathing in deeply, I feel my mind free and alive. Breathing out slowly, I feel my mind free and alive.

8. Breathing in deeply, I see freedom for all people. Breathing out slowly, I see freedom for all people.
9. Breathing in deeply, I feel healed and whole. Breathing out slowly, I feel healed and whole.
10. Breathing in deeply, I see all people healed and whole. Breathing out slowly, I see all people healed and whole.
11. Breathing in deeply, I let go of my expectations and fears. Breathing out slowly, I let go of my expectations and fears.
12. Breathing in deeply, I am aware that I'm breathing in deeply. Breathing out slowly, I am aware that I'm breathing out slowly.

99

Breath circles

Do four inhales and exhales through the nose without any
  stopping or pausing.

Then take one long inhale through the nose to the count of five
  and one long exhale to the count of five.

Merge the inhale and the exhale into a circle. Actually feel your
  breathing move in a circular motion.

Then repeat the sequence four more times.

Wake-up call: healing

Pain, ironically, will be your true and only path to healing.
You always start where you are, so at times you should
begin by offering healing to yourself for the piece of
suffering that is right in your face. Stopping, calming,
and resting are preconditions for healing. Healing requires
receptivity and acceptance. None of it can be forced.
You have to create the right conditions and then let go.
The process of healing begins when you acknowledge
your suffering and explore it, when you admit what is
happening and accept it.

100

BREATH AS LIGHTHOUSE

Another way to view your breath is as a lighthouse. It helps you know exactly where you are, even in a raging storm. Your breath is like a spiritual lighthouse guiding you back to the present moment.

No matter what your emotional condition is, following the lighthouse will help you arrive safely in the present moment.

Welcome this moment when you can apply the brakes, take a deep breath, and gather yourself at this landmark before proceeding anew.

Feel each in-breath calm your body and mind and each out-breath release any tension or thoughts you are holding. Stay with this exercise for 10–15 minutes.

101

Bellows breath

*If you have any respiratory or cardiac issues, please use caution or skip this exercise.

Sit in a cross-legged position. Rapidly inhale and exhale up to 10 times through your nose, short and fast. Keep the in- and out-breaths equal in strength and length.

Afterward, take one deep breath in, rest your chin on your chest, and hold.

Then raise your head and exhale.

Do this for 2 rounds per sitting. This stimulating breath will raise vital energy and increase alertness.

102

SPACIOUS BREATHING

You can stand unmindfully in line at the fast-food restaurant or
you can be meditating—focusing on your breathing and your
whole-body presence. Whenever you have your attention
on the here and now, perceiving your inner and outer reality
without judging it, you are meditating.

Practicing spacious breathing allows you to observe deep-rooted
patterns of tension in various postures and movements of your
body, patterns that inhibit the sensation of energy and movement.

You may lie down, sit, or be standing for this exercise.

Let your belly soften and expand as you inhale through your nose,
breathing in deeply all the way from your belly up through
your chest. Feel your breath expanding your belly, solar plexus,
and chest.

Slowly release your breath through your nose, expelling as much
air as you comfortably can.

Repeat this cycle for 5 minutes or longer. Develop a natural
rhythm without forcing it.

Systematic rhythmic breathing done at your own pace oxygenates
and cleanses your mind and body.

103

BREATHING WITH WATER SOUNDS

On a rainy day, find a sheltered place outside or sit inside by an
open window. Look at the rain falling down from the sky.
Appreciate how important it is to have rain.

Close your eyes and breathe deeply three times.

Become present with the natural sounds of the water on objects
like leaves, roads, and structures. Listen.

Focus on the sounds. Alternatively, you can focus on the smells.

Breathe in and out, calming the body and mind, for as long as you
comfortably can, 5–20 minutes.

Wake-up call: hearing

There is a big difference between hearing someone and
listening to someone. Take away your opinions and what
is left? Take away your opinion of your condition and
situation and your mind is clear like space—and you will hear
clearly. Aim to be constructive, positive, empathetic. Give
support and encouragement. Be open and sensitive to what
others are experiencing and you will truly hear them.

104

AH EXHALING

Stand up, feet hip-width apart. Relax.

Take 5 deep belly breaths through the nose.

Then breathe into any part of your body that is tense or stressed, visualizing a stream of light massaging away the tension. Relax. Each breath will be like fingers massaging away the tension and stress.

Exhale and let out an AH each time.

We need to loosen our armor, breathe a little more freely.

Continue this exercise for each part of your body until you feel totally loose and free.

105

ENOUGH

Breathe in and say to yourself, "What I have is enough."

Breathe out and say, "What I am is enough."

Breathe in and say, "What I do is enough."

Breathe out and say, "What I have achieved is enough."

Repeat this for several minutes. In this crazed world, you need to let up on your expectations, especially of yourself. You can use the breath in this exercise to help you cultivate appreciation and compassion toward your efforts and accomplishments. Most of the time what you have, are, do, and have achieved is enough.

106

RELAXING SIGH

A sigh releases a bit of tension and can be practiced as a means of relaxing.

Sit in a chair or stand straight. Relax. Inhale deeply through the nose.

Sigh deeply, letting out a sound of deep relief as air rushes out your lungs and out your mouth. Or exhale through a puckered O mouth.

Let new air come in naturally through the nose.

Do this 3–12 times whenever you feel the need for it. Sigh.

107

LIQUID FLOW

For 3 minutes, lie in the relaxation pose. Lie down on your back, your arms slightly out from your sides, palms up. Your legs should be separate and fall open, relaxed. Your eyes should be closed.

Sense your whole body, especially the points where it touches the surface you are lying on.

Scan your body, relaxing each part as you come to it.

This is preparation for breath awareness. You will be focusing on receiving your inhalations.

Imagine that all the doors of every cell of your body are opened by the incoming breath.

For 5–10 minutes, soften as you inhale and let breath fill you naturally.

Imagine that your body is full of liquid and as you inhale the liquid flows down into the rise of your belly.

As you exhale, imagine the liquid flowing from your lower abdomen toward your nose.

Do this for 5–10 minutes.

108

Free breathing

Understand the characteristics of free breathing: the whole body oscillates, the breath arises through the diaphragm, the breath arises from within, the breath expands in all directions, the breath is calm and regular.

Find a quiet and relaxing place to either sit or stand to practice free breathing.

Partake in quiet respiration: 2 seconds inhale, 3 seconds exhale, followed by a pause.

The breathing out is a little longer than breathing in.

In free breathing, the breath has variations and is adaptable—it's effortless and relaxed.

Experience this for 10–20 cycles.

109

LETTING GO

Sitting cross-legged or in a chair, half-smile.

Inhale and exhale deeply through your nose.

Maintain this half-smile.

Let go at the end of the out-breath, letting the thoughts go. It is like moving a boulder away so that water can keep flowing. Your energy and life force will be able to evolve and go forward, like the water you just released, when you let go.

Let go for 20 minutes.

The next time you feel your spirits sagging, practice this half-smile for 20–30 minutes and notice how you feel.

110

In the garden

Go to a garden and just stand in it.

Breathe in the air, the fragrances, the light, the temperature, the music of the plant and animal life in the garden. Breathe out through your mouth the carbon dioxide that helps sustain the plants.

Inhale the prana (cosmic energy) of these growing things. Feel nature enter you with every breath in.

Recharge your inner batteries for 15–20 minutes.

Rapid count breathing

Sit in a comfortable position. Relax. Focus your mind on
your breathing.

Breathe in through your nose while counting rapidly to 10 and
breathe out through your nose while counting rapidly to 10.

While counting 1, 2, 3, 4, 5, 6, 7, 8, 9, 10, breathe in through
your nose.

While counting 1, 2, 3, 4, 5, 6, 7, 8, 9, 10, breathe out through
your nose.

Repeat this as many times as necessary to focus your mind on
the breath.

Breath of Fire

The breath of fire is a rapid inhalation and exhalation through your nose that strengthens your nervous system and energizes you. Air is pulled in and pumped out rhythmically, like pumping a bellows. There is no tension in the abdominal, chest, or rib cage muscles. It is actually fairly effortless.

The flow of the breath soothes the mind and allows for steadiness and relaxation.

Be seated or you can stand for this exercise. Start with long deep breathing in and out through your nose. Feel your lungs expanding.

Then as soon as the lungs are completely expanded, immediately force the air out.

As soon as most of the air is out, immediately expand the air back in. Breath of fire is done through the nose and the inhalation and exhalation are of equal duration. The body stays relatively still and relaxed, only the naval point is vigorously working.

You will feel the diaphragm filling the lungs from the back to the front completely, then contracting again.

With each breath one expands a bit faster and contracts a bit faster until without expanding or contracting completely, a rhythm is felt, and you let that rhythm take over.

Do 20 short puffs in and out. You can contract the belly to help expel the breath. After this, take a few normal breaths.

Wake-up call: helpfulness

Change your attitude by becoming helpful. Ask yourself: will what I do or say be helpful? You can align your speech to the principles of what is truthful and what is most helpful. If a speech act is motivated by true helpfulness, it will bring a positive result. Take a few days to carefully notice the intentions that motivate your speech. Direct your attention to the state of mind that precedes talking, the motivation for your comments, responses, and observations. Try to be particularly aware of whether your speech is even subtly motivated by boredom, concern, irritation, loneliness, compassion, fear, love, competitiveness, greed, hate, etc. Be aware of the general mood or state of your heart and mind and how it may be influencing your speech. The goal in becoming helpful is to think kindly and speak gently and clearly.

113

Remember to Breathe

When you realize you are under stress or overwhelmed, simply remind yourself to breathe. Once you realize that you are again in control of your breath, your breathing will become more rhythmic and slower.

Become aware of your breathing.

Let your breath quiet your mind and re-center yourself.

Take a deep breath, filling your lungs, then exhale in quick snorts, rapidly contracting and releasing your stomach muscles.

Do this for a minute or two to oxygenate the blood and raise prana (the life force) in your system. This can be very helpful in the many stressful situations we face.

114

THE 4–16–8 BREATH

Sit quietly. Relax. Become aware of your breathing.

Inhale through your nose for 4 counts, hold for 16, exhale through your nose for 8.

When you are new to this exercise, you can inhale through your nose for a 1 count, hold for 4, exhale through your nose for 2. You will soon be able to increase your count.

Do three sets of 10 at least once a day.

THREE BREATHING SPACES

Sit comfortably. Relax. To help open the three breathing spaces,
   press the appropriate finger pads of one hand against those of
   the other. The three breathing spaces are your neck/throat,
   your chest/diaphragm, and your belly/abdomen.

To help open the lower breathing space, press the pads of the little
   fingers and pads of the ring fingers together firmly.

For the middle space, press the middle fingers together.

For the upper breathing space, press the pads of the thumbs and
   index fingers together.

Take up to 8 full breaths while pressing together any combination.

116

SOUNDS INSIDE YOU

Most of the time we only think of the sounds that exist in the external world.

Instead, relax into the breath and listen for sounds inside of you, including inside the space between your ears.

Try allowing the sounds of your inner world to come to you for 5 minutes or more.

Wake-up call: honesty

The vast majority of problems in relationships come from communications that lack honesty. You need to regularly stop and ask yourself if you are moving in the direction of more honesty or not. Speaking honestly needs to be linked to a heart of kindness and compassion. In relationships, you have a special opportunity. If you practice consistently saying what is true in an honest and loving way, again and again over time, it can bring about deep changes for the other person as well as for you. Any gesture of honesty and seeing clearly will affect how you experience your world. What you do for yourself you also do for others, and what you do for others, you do for yourself.

117

LETTING GO OF PAIN

Find a comfortable place to sit or lie down.

Place one hand on your stomach right above your belly button.
Place your other hand in the middle of your chest on top of
your breastbone. Take a breath. Notice how it feels.

Breathe deeply. You should be able to first feel your hand on your
stomach and then your other hand rise as your lungs fill with air.

Hold each breath briefly, then slowly breathe out. Feel your
abdomen and chest slowly lower as you breathe out.

Notice the air entering your nose and mouth. Imagine the air
going in your nose and mouth and filling your lungs. Notice
the hand on your stomach slowly rise.

Try to make your breaths longer and slower.

As you breathe, let the air surround all the tension or pain that
you feel in your body.
Imagine that you are blowing pain and tension out of your body
as the air leaves your mouth.

Continue breathing and focus your mind and breathing on the
tense or painful areas.

118

LIP PURSING BREATH

Perform this next to a window or outside. Get yourself in a comfortable position, either sitting or standing.

Purse your lips as though you are going to whistle, then inhale slowly through your mouth to the count of seven.

Pause for one count.

Then softly exhale through both nostrils to the count of seven.

Repeat this six times.

Practice lip pursing breath in the morning and at noon. It is a great way to get you focused for the day and to increase energy for the afternoon.

119

FALLING ASLEEP

While lying comfortably in your bed and getting ready for sleep,
focus on your breath. Breathe normally in and out through
your nose.

Note the speed of your breaths. Try to steady your breathing
before continuing with the exercise.

Then transfer your awareness to your heart. You may be aware of it
beating or you may just focus on the space of the heart.

Visualize and try to sense the presence of a disk of still white light
with its center at the heart and its circumference extending a
little beyond the heart.

Set the disk spinning, slowly and then faster. As it spins, you can see
a rainbow of colors and their merging to form the white light.

Fall asleep with the disk still spinning.

BREATHING A HALF–SMILE

When you realize that you are irritated, half-smile right away.

Inhale and exhale quietly, maintaining a half-smile for 3 breaths.

As you inhale through your nose, you can draw the yin energy of the earth, a powerful healing energy, through your feet and upward into your body. Keep the half-smile.

As you exhale, you can direct any toxic or stagnant energies downward to your feet and out into the earth. Is that half-smile still there?

Be mindful when breathing, "I am inhaling and exhaling and following each from beginning to end."

Sometimes it is difficult to relax into the breath and surrender if you forget the half-smile. Once you learn to smile to your breath, this exercise will calm you.

Breathe with a half-smile for 10–20 minutes.

The inward-directed smile is like a beam of energy that guides the spacious breath deeper into you. The spacious breath is like a wave that moves the energy of the smile to all parts of you.

121

Every half hour

If you want to develop attention, you can decide that you
 will pause each half hour and come back to your breath.
 Concentrate on your breath for a minute or two. Keep your
 breathing relaxed.

You can do this exercise while at your desk at work, shopping,
 driving, or relaxing. You can aim to do it all day long!

Wake-up call: humility

Real humility is saying, "I did the best I could," "I am not
perfect," and "I do not know." When you honestly try
as hard as you can at something, admit your wrongs,
don't seek perfection, and realize you do not have all the
answers, you find humility. The greeting and farewell,
Namaste, means, "I recognize the light in you" or "I honor
the divinity in you," and indicates respect and humility.

122

Join inhaling and exhaling

This exercise has you join inhaling and exhaling instead of thinking of them as separate.

Empty the lungs, mentally counting "one." Count both inhalation and exhalation as one.

Inhale, exhale, and count "two."

This should be done only up to five and then repeated five to one.

Repeat this method until your breathing becomes refined and quiet, a minimum of 5 minutes. Feel your mind and body recharged.

123

SQUEEZE OUT STALE AIR

Lie on your back. Relax.

Exhale through your nose and stretch the spine, tipping your
tailbone/pelvis up toward the ceiling while squeezing out
stale air.

When the air is squeezed out, let the inhale come naturally.
Breathe in through your nose. Feel your body relax.

Repeat 12 times.

Wake-up call: humor

A sense of humor helps you lighten up and not take
things too seriously. You can choose to do your
job and live your life with a healthy sense of humor.
Always look for the humor in your situation. Unless you
learn to laugh at yourself, you will never be completely
without delusion.

124

Attend to the breath

Close your eyes. Begin selectively to attend to the breath.

During the in-breath, confine your attention to those aspects of the body that are contractive, such as the tightening of your diaphragm. Pull in and collapse on the in-breath. Contract down to an effortless nothingness.

Bring the attention to your out-breath. During this part of the cycle, confine your attention to those qualities of feelings and sensations that are expansive.

Your experience expands with the out-breath and contracts with the in-breath. Do this for 5–10 minutes.

Then, open your eyes.

Try to bring this quality of calm awareness to your next activity.

125

ZAZEN MUDRA

Sit and keep your eyes cast on the floor about three to four feet in front of your body, eyes neither fully opened nor closed; like a relaxed squint. Keep your lips and teeth together with your tongue resting against the roof of your mouth.

Place your hands on your lap with the right palm up and your left hand (palm up) resting on your right hand, thumb-tips lightly touching, forming a horizontal oval. This is the zazen mudra. Zazen is attending to an experience as it presents itself with the whole body-mind. The hand placement, the mudra, is the "gesture of reality" and will help you to notice how you are. This practice helps you be aware of whatever mental state arises as it arises.

Place the sides of the little fingers against your abdomen, a few inches below the navel, harmonizing your center of gravity with the mudra.

Take a few deep breaths, exhaling fully. Let your breath settle into its natural rhythm. Sit still and keep your attention on your breath.

When your attention wanders, bring it back to the breath again and again, as many times as necessary. Be fully present for 15–20 minutes.

At the end of your sitting period, gently sway your body from right to left. Stretch out your legs.

126

RETAINING BREATH

Close your eyes. Take some conscious deep breaths, then take in a deep breath and hold it and bring your chin down.

Then raise the head and exhale through your nose.

Be awake to the continually changing tones of the breath. Be awake to the blessing of the air flowing in and the air flowing out. Accept each in-breath as the beginning. Accept each out-breath as letting go.

Do this 1–5 cycles.

Wake-up call: imagination

Let your imagination work with no expectations, exercising and nourishing it. Frank Lloyd Wright wrote that "An idea is salvation by imagination" and Henry David Thoreau said, "The world is but a canvas to imagination." Consider a tropical fish in an aquarium: he believes that the ocean is a ten-second swim from one glassy rock-face to another. We are all conditioned by our circumstances to believe that our lives are typical. Let your imagination rove, and find new possibilities for yourself.

127

RED LIGHT OR STOP SIGN

When you are waiting at a red light or standing there impatiently trying to get the toaster to work faster, wake up! You can use a red light or anything else that makes you wait as a signal of mindfulness, reminding you to stop and enjoy your breathing.

Create a "red light" or "stop sign" practice out of this type of experience. During the minutes that you are waiting for the red light to change or the toaster is doing its thing, just breathe and calm yourself.

Waiting for the red light to change or the toast is an opportunity for you to experience peace. You can use this for the many situations in which you feel impatient.

Once you develop this practice, then any other time when you are nervous, edgy, jumpy, overwrought, or otherwise on edge, you will know to take the time to follow your breath.

Take deep slow breaths while on the phone, in the car, or waiting for something or someone.

Breathe, smile, and settle into the present moment.

128

HEAD TO FEET

Stand with knees slightly bent and feet parallel and shoulder width apart. Let your arms and shoulders relax.

Breathing in through your nose, allow your inhalation to rise from your feet and go up and out through the top of your head.

You may sense your spine being lengthened and your head being pulled upward to rest lightly on your spine.

Breathing out, allow your exhalation to start from the top of your head and move down through your feet into the earth.

Make your peace on each breath for 10–20 minutes.

129

RELAXATION BUTTON

Create a "relaxation button" that you can use in your daily life
to calm yourself and control your emotions. Athletes do this
before they get up to the plate in baseball or shoot a foul shot
in basketball or putt a golf ball.

Practice using a breathing technique and in your mind pair it with
an event of daily life like answering the phone or responding to a
child's demand. You can then "set" this event as a relaxation button
when you will relax and practice using a breathing technique.

Breathing in through your nose, be aware of the activities of your
mind being calm and at peace.

Breathing out, be aware of the activities of your mind being calm
and at peace.

We have to learn the art of breathing in and out, stopping our
activities, and calming our emotions. We have to learn to
become solid and stable like an oak tree, not blown side to
side by a storm.

130

Thirty-second meditations

When you do not even have two minutes, you will find that just 30 seconds of meditation a few times a day can transform your experience of life. It is a classic case of a little bit going a long way.

Be aware of the sensation of the breath, but breathe normally. If you simply pause long enough to remember to be aware of your breathing and say, "I am breathing freely," this quick expansion into full breath awareness will awaken your whole-body consciousness.

You transform your day for the better when you are aware of your breathing. It does not matter what you are doing or who you are with. No one needs to know what you are up to.

Just take 30 seconds a few times each day to tune in to your breathing and the present moment.

131

OM

Inhale, silently saying OM (ohm).

Mentally see that the oxygen coming into your body is filled with life-force energy and hold the breath in your mouth.

Force the air against your cheeks and let them fill to capacity and bulge out. Keep pressing the air into your cheeks as long as you comfortably can.

Then discharge your breath quickly and forcefully through the mouth.

As you do this, further imagine that your breath is revitalizing every cell in your body.

Do this cycle 8–10 times.

132

Wake-up smile

Put a sticky note or a sign that says SMILE somewhere where
you'll see it when you open your eyes in the morning. It will be
your reminder.

Relax and use the seconds before you get out of bed to breathe.
Inhale and exhale 3 breaths gently through your nose while
maintaining a half-smile. Become aware of your breathing and
the half-smile with each breath.

After this exercise, continue to lie on your bed and take a few
minutes to feel the effects of your practice before you continue
your day.

Wake-up call: impermanence

Impermanence is a principle of harmony. Everything in life
is in a constant state of flux. When you do not struggle
against it, you are in harmony with reality. You must use
every precious moment. Be aware of impermanence and
appreciate the enormous potential of your human existence.

133

Meeting a holy person

Sit comfortably with your eyes closed, like you are getting ready to meet a holy person. Watch the breath going in and out of the nose like a visitor.

Know what it is doing, keep following it, while simultaneously awakening the mind.

Eventually the breath disappears altogether and all that remains is the feeling of wakefulness.

This is called meeting a holy person.

Do this exercise for 10–15 minutes.

134

Snakelike breathing

Put your tongue between your lips and stick it out slightly.

Inhale through your mouth while producing a snakelike hissing sound.

When your lungs feel full, hold the breath as long as possible.

Then slowly exhale with both nostrils.

Practice this five times in the morning, at noon, and at night.

135

STRAW BREATHING

You can recline or sit on a cushion or chair. Place a long straw in your mouth and hold it with your hand.

Breathe in through your nose and then breathe out through the straw in your mouth. Work gently so you do not push the breath out.

To assist breathing in through your nose, lightly touch your tongue to the roof of your mouth.

What you want to happen is for the inhalation to arise spontaneously, feeling like a gentle bounce up through the center of your body.

As you exhale, let the exhalation take place naturally and gently only through the straw. Do not use force as you exhale. Just exhale in a relaxed, natural way, being sure that the air leaves only through the straw, not through your nose (which you can pinch closed).

When your exhalation is almost complete, take the straw out of your mouth, close your mouth, finish your exhalation in a natural, relaxed way through your nose, and then simply wait for the inhalation to occur on its own.

After using the straw for one exhalation, just breathe normally without the straw for 2 or 3 breaths through your nose, letting your breath settle by itself into a natural rhythm.

Then, inhale through your nose again, return the straw to your mouth, and repeat the entire process.

Do this for 3 minutes total.

Wake-up call: insight

Insight into the true nature of reality is the ultimate secret of lasting peace and happiness. For insight to develop, a spirit of observation and deep questioning must be kept in the forefront. Recognizing what you do with your mind, how not present you often are, and how delicious whatever you are doing can be—these insights make even the most mundane activities delightful and nourishing.

136

SLOWING THE MIND

Our minds are always racing. You need to acknowledge that thinking nonstop is a strong habit for you. It happens to everyone. One of the best things we can do to improve every aspect of our lives is to give the mind a chance to rest. Even if only done for a few moments each day, it will be helpful.

The easiest way to give the mind a break is to learn to focus on your breathing in a sitting position for a short time, just 5–10 breaths. Sit comfortably and relax.

Control the strength of the inhalation and exhalation so it is slow and steady.

Do this for 5–10 breaths every time you feel you need it.

137

Exhale to sleep

As you go to bed and prepare for sleep, take some mindful breaths, become aware of the bed supporting you, and allow yourself to smile.

Feel the muscles of your body relaxing with each inhalation and exhalation as you sink into your bed.

Make each exhalation before bed profoundly deep. Let everything go.

You could also make the exhalation twice as long as the inhalation.

Breathe out the ego.

Become aware of your breathing and of what feelings or thoughts are passing through you.

Good night!

138

EXERCISE BREATHING

Go running or walking and coordinate your breath with your steps. For example, coordinate your breathing so that you inhale with four steps, then exhale with four steps.

The first step, when you run or walk, is to figure out the length of your breath (inhalation and exhalation) by the number of your footsteps. While inhaling, count the number of steps you take. Do the same while exhaling.

Let inhalation be natural.

Do this for 10 breaths.

How far can you go before you lose track of the breath?

This is a surprising lesson!

Then lengthen the exhalation by one more footstep. Only lengthen the inhalation when you feel good about doing so.

Do this for 20 breaths. Then breathe normally for the duration of the walk or run.

139

Mindful Waiting

Use what might otherwise be considered "wasted" or "dead" time (e.g., in your car, waiting for an appointment, waiting in line) to focus your awareness on your immediate experience.

Do standing meditation while waiting in line for a movie or bus or train. Just stand there, breathe, and awaken. Nice, steady breaths. Become more aware of your immediate experience with each breath.

The second you choose to mind your breath, you have decided that this present moment is worthy of your full attention.

Use your breath as the object of concentration.

Doing this will help you to expand the sense of presence and connection to your everyday activities and experiences.

May each breath bring you back to the home of yourself during your waiting time.

140

Meditative Walking

Meditating while you walk is a pleasant, easy way to expand your powers of concentration since the practice requires no accessories and no quiet room or special circumstance.

You can focus on your breathing and count out your breaths while walking. Inhale through your nose and take a step. Exhale through your mouth or nose and take another step.

Just break your steps down into slow, mindful movements and breathe.

You may repeat a favorite inspirational verse or affirmation as you walk.

Notice how the ground rises up to meet your feet. Do this for around 20–60 minutes.

141

Going to sleep

Lie down in the relaxation pose in bed, on your back, legs separate and relaxed, arms out a little ways from your torso with the palms up.

Breathe in through your nose and imagine your body being filled with more light and space. Breathe out.

Melt into this ocean of light and space and fall asleep peacefully.

Wake-up call: integrity

Someone who regularly practices kind and helpful speech develops integrity, and this gives speech, and even silence, a certain power that cannot be measured, but is felt. When in doubt about what to say, silence preserves integrity.

FAVORITE COLOR

Use a cue, like every time you see your favorite color, to pause and feel the moment between your inhalation and your exhalation.

It's that simple. You will also be amazed at how often you see your favorite color.

Wake-up call: intention

Practice consciously doing one thing at a time. Do whatever you are doing more slowly and more intentionally. The possibility of transforming yourself rests in your intentions to awaken. When you are aware of your intentions in the present, you can shape your future. What you are doing will be more satisfying and enjoyable.

143

HALF SUN SALUTE

Stand in the mountain pose, erect like a string is pulling you up from the scalp, arms at your sides with the palms turned forward for balance and alignment.

Take deep breaths through your nose, raising your arms over your head, and touch your palms.

Then fold forward from the hips, exhaling into a swan dive into a forward bend.

On an inhalation, lengthen the spine and lift the heart away from the floor, keeping your fingertips touching the floor, your knees, or your shins.

Then, as you exhale, fold back into a forward bend again.

Let the inhalation swoop you up to standing, arms sweeping out to the side, and palms coming together overhead.

Then let your arms float down on the exhalation, drawing the palms together in a prayer position at your heart.

Breathe in and out three times, refreshing yourself through awareness.

Do 3–10 half sun salutes.

144

CHAKRA BREATHING

Consciously direct your breathing to each of the seven chakras,
spending 2 minutes at each energy center. Practice this process
once a day for a week, and notice how your mind-body shifts.
Once you have the process down, it can be done in less than
5 minutes. When you are first beginning, use 2 minutes for
each chakra.

Using your mind, try to sense the chakra at the base of your spine
or perineum (sex/earth chakra). You can imagine it as a lotus
flower or as a spinning wheel or storehouse of energy. Sense
the energy. Breathe naturally.

Move up to the next chakra in the lower abdomen, two inches
below your navel, just above your genital area (sacral/water
chakra). Feel its energy. You can breathe energy into the
chakra, revitalizing it.

Move up to the chakra in the solar plexus/navel (solar plexus/
fire chakra).

Then the heart chakra (heart/wind chakra). Continue to follow
the breath.

Then the throat chakra. Continue deep breathing, expanding the
area of the throat.

Then the forehead between the eyes (third eye chakra).
Maintain awareness.

Finally, the top of your head (crown chakra). Allow the breath to open the top of your skull.

Pay attention. Smile!

Wake-up call: interconnectedness

Loving-friendliness, a sense of interconnectedness with all beings and a sincere wish for them to be happy, has far-reaching effects. Try to find the blessing of inner silence and peace, and mindfully speak to and listen for interconnectedness between yourself and others.

Wake-up call: interest

If a person is genuinely interested in achieving happiness, then that person does not need sophisticated machines or material wealth. The happiest people are those who think the most interesting thoughts. Those who decide to use leisure as a means of mental development, who love good music, good books, good pictures, good company, good conversation, are the happiest people in the world. And they are not only happy in themselves, they are the cause of happiness in others.

145

BREATHING AWAY A CRAVING

If you can inhale and hold 7 breaths, your oxygen will be
completely circulated through your blood system, and you
shall not need whatever you were craving/longing to have.

Sit and inhale through your nose but exhale through your mouth.

Your mouth should be mostly closed and the exhalation is slow,
quiet, and steady.

Allow the air in your lungs to be fully exhaled before inhaling
again. Do this 7 times for one set. Your oxygen will be
completely circulated through your blood system.

Breathe quietly this way for 5–10 minutes or for 20 sets of
7 breaths.

Wake-up call: intimacy

Intimacy is an experience of non-separation, of being at
one with whatever is happening. Wise speech has the
power to heal division and to foster love and trust, which
leads to intimacy.

146

SENSE OF HEARING

Waiting? Standing in line? Bring your attention to your
breath. Listen!

Close your eyes and focus on the sounds of your breathing to
refresh your sense of hearing and your ability to concentrate.
Inhale through your nose, listen to the sound it makes.
Concentrate on this noise. Exhale. Again, listen to the sound it
makes and concentrate on this noise. Inhale and exhale deeper
with each breath while focusing on the sound. It may be the
only thing you hear.

You can use this same exercise to make a conscious effort to relax
your breathing during conversations. Listening is a great gift
you give to others.

Welcome those moments when you can take a deep breath and
gather yourself before proceeding anew. No matter what else
is happening around you, focusing on the sounds of your
breathing will refresh you.

147

DIGESTIVE BREATHING

Sit on a chair with your spine erect but relaxed, hands on your knees with fingers pointed downward.

Fit your index finger, middle finger, and ring finger into the indentations of each knee. With slight pressure, these fingers are stimulating the meridians running through the knees.

Inhale energy gently into your expanding belly.

Exhale and let your belly naturally contract.

Inhale through your nose. Your exhale can be through the nose or mouth.

Do this for 5 minutes after each meal or whenever you have digestive problems.

Wake-up call: karma

There are three doors—thought, speech, actions—with which karma is made. If an unskillful thought arises, be careful that it does not turn into speech or action. Our thoughts are our karma. Our likes and dislikes, opinions, concepts—which drive us to speech and action—create more karma.

148

Tuning the Breath

When you do this breathing exercise, you are "tuning" the breath, strengthening the muscles involved in breathing and gaining respiratory control.

Lie on your back. Relax. Breathe evenly and gently, focusing your attention on the movement of your belly.

As you breathe in, let your belly rise in order to bring air into the lower half of your lungs.

As the upper half of your lungs fill with air, your chest will rise and your belly will begin to lower.

As you breathe out, squeeze a bit to get the last of the air out of the belly. After a few cycles, lengthen the exhale.

Do this for 10 cycles.

149

FILLING THE LUNGS

Sit or lie down in a comfortable position. Relax your body.

Try breathing in a long breath through your nose and, when the lungs are full, count "one."

Then breathe out completely, counting "two."

Continue this up to 10. How do you feel?

Repeat this exercise for as long as you like.

Wake-up call: kindness

Life is so hard, how can we be anything but kind? Everyone can learn from your kindness and everyone deserves your kindness. Becoming a more loving person in your everyday relationships may be one of the most compassionate actions you can do. Become a little kinder.

BREATH PERCEPTION

As you move through your day, carry an inner sense of openness and wholeness with you.

Use the breath to help you renew this sense. The breath is key to everything within us.

Train your mind to pay attention to the space and distance between things.

Train your perception to experience how space connects everything.

Let every inhalation root you more firmly in your strong self and every exhalation rid you of worries and insecurities.

Wake-up call: learning

Learn from whatever presents itself. Your life always presents what you need to learn. Whether you stay home or work in an office or whatever, the next teacher is going to pop right up. Recognize it and learn from it. And if learning is not followed by reflecting and practicing, it is not true learning.

151

OOO BURSTS

Sit comfortably. Form the syllable "OOO" with your lips.

Inhale through your mouth in 7 small bursts.

Swallow the 7 breaths.

Exhale through both nostrils, counting to 7.

Repeat 24 times in the morning and evening over a week's time.
    Feel yourself become more alert and energized.

Wake-up call: letting go

Practice letting go and you will cultivate inner peace.
Practice fully experiencing what is happening in each
moment with as much awareness as possible, not wanting
it to be different than it is. Then, whatever is happening—
good, bad, or indifferent—let it go.

COMPASSIONATE BEING BREATHING

Begin in a comfortable position. Close your eyes and imagine the most loving and compassionate individuals you have ever known or heard about.

These compassionate beings are gathered over your head and merge into one being who glows and radiates the warmth and light of love and compassion.

Imagine that this being descends into your heart, where it takes the form of a sphere of infinitely radiant compassionate light that merges with your soft spot.

On the inhalation, breathe in any negativity or darkness and take it into the sphere of light in your heart, transforming it.

On the exhalation, breathe positive qualities into your mind and feel them purifying it.

Breathe in the dark and breathe out the light for some time. You will shine like a beacon of light from a lighthouse.

Do this exercise for 10–20 minutes.

153

Very interesting

Breathe in. Rest in the arisen breath.

Note the space, the pause. Rest in the not-yet-arisen breath.

See if you can rest in that space between breaths.

Exhale gently. Note the space, the pause.

There is a sense of ease that comes from letting the breath just happen.

Stick with this for 10 minutes.

When you start to see the spaces, the breath will become very interesting!

Wake-up call: listening

When you learn to become more open, you have the possibility of listening in stillness. Speech is most beautiful when it approaches silence. You can learn to listen to the stillness behind the words, others words, and the words in your mind.

154

AWARENESS OF TIME MEDITATION

Note what time it is as you sit and relax, breathing deeply.

Close your eyes and focus on your breath.

Sit for as long as you feel comfortable.

Before you open your eyes, guess the time spent in meditation.

When you look at your watch or clock, you may be surprised at your underestimation or overestimation.

If you are correct, do not be pleased. If you are incorrect, do not be disappointed. The object of this exercise is to increase awareness.

Wake-up call: love

The first step to understanding and feeling love is to generate love for yourself. Do not judge yourself harshly. Without mercy for yourself, you cannot love others and the world. The more love you can extend, the more people you can include in it, the more love you have. Love is discovered when you stop indulging in self-centeredness, fear, and anger.

155

EVERY MOVEMENT

Thích Nhất Hạnh suggests combining awareness of your
breathing with every movement of your body: "Breathing in,
I am sitting down." "Breathing out, I am cleaning the table."
"Breathing in, I smile to myself."

He says that stopping the random progression of thoughts and no
longer living in forgetfulness are giant steps forward. It does
not matter how many times you have to remind yourself to be
aware of your breathing.

The way to do this is by following your breath and combining
it with awareness of each daily activity. This cultivates
concentration and living in an awakened state.

Wake-up call: *loving-kindness*

When you are guided by loving-kindness, you are able
to look deeply into the heart of reality and see the
truth. When you smile a smile of compassion, you are
encouraging your loving-kindness to wake up. Say, "May
I be well. May I be peaceful and at ease. May I be happy."
These are aspects to loving-kindness. Repeat for others
you know.

156

LIQUID LIGHT

Imagine a pool deep in the earth that is a source of vitality and energy.

Breathing in, you feel the liquid light rise like a fountain into your feet, up the legs, into the spine, and to the top of your head.

Breathing out, the energy cascades back to the ground and you feel cleansed.

Stay with this exercise for around 10 minutes.

Wake-up call: loyalty

The Japanese term *bushido*, meaning "way of the warrior," refers to the tradition of respect and devotion between samurai, including absolute loyalty to the master, discipline, self-restraint, and a willingness to sacrifice oneself. Bring something of the samurai's dedication and loyalty to the values you deem to be important.

157

Happy Lion

As you prepare to start your day, envision a large happy lion
stretching and roaring.

Raise your arms and spread them wide with the palms forward.

Stretch. Breathe. Repeat!

Like the happy lion, leap forward and roar into your day.

Wake-up call: meditation

The breath is always available and always simple, making
it the best anchor for meditation. Focusing on the breath
calms the mind and provides the stability necessary for
you to cultivate concentration. You will be studying
its nuances and how it changes, and it will teach you
awareness of the present moment. When thoughts
or images arise in the mind, as soon as you become
aware of this, make a soft mental note of "thinking" or
"wandering" or "seeing." Notice when you become aware
of the thought or image—without judgment. Be mindful
of where your mind has gone, then let the thoughts or
images go and return to the breath.

158

Breathing through panic

If you are feeling panicked in a situation, make a conscious effort to calm down.

Instruct yourself to stop, then close your eyes and breathe slowly and deeply. Make sure the inhalations and exhalations are comfortable for you.

Feel yourself becoming more relaxed and your heartbeat slowing down. Be in control of the pace of your breathing.

Practice conscious breathing and smiling. While you practice this conscious breathing, also put a smile on your face. Relax the cheeks and smile.

The combination of breathing and smiling will keep you steady by helping you balance. If conscious breathing is your anchor, smiling is your balance point. You need to combine the two in order to reduce your panic.

Do this for 10–20 minutes until you start to feel more calm.

159

Breathe through smile

Sit in a comfortable position and close your eyes. Relax. Sense
your face breathing through your smile.

On the inhale, sense the air entering through your nose, but also
through your face and eyes.

Let your natural smile and breath touch. The smile transforms
your breathing. You may notice an increase in saliva and this is
a good thing. Saliva is sometimes called "the golden elixir" and
contains many substances that aid your overall health.

As you exhale, feel the air emitting from your nose, eyes, mouth,
and face.

Try breathing through your smiling face for 5 minutes.

160

BALANCING-THE-SELF MEDITATION

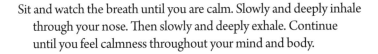

Sit and watch the breath until you are calm. Slowly and deeply inhale
through your nose. Then slowly and deeply exhale. Continue
until you feel calmness throughout your mind and body.

If you are right-handed, concentrate on the left side of your body,
particularly your left hand and foot. Do the opposite if you are
left-handed.

Visualize yourself walking toward a door. Imagine reaching out
with your left hand and turning the handle. (Do the opposite if
you are left-handed.)

In your mind, begin to walk through the doorway, being mindful
of taking the first step with your left foot. (If you are left-
handed, step with the right foot.)

As you pass through the doorway, turn toward the left and close
the door with your left hand. (Opposite for a lefty.)

Once you have finished the visualization, imagine powerful
energy coursing up your left side.

Do this visualization slowly. It should take at least 10–20 minutes.

Try to bring this increased awareness into your life after
the meditation.

161

Attentive gap

Whatever you are doing, wherever you are, keep attentive to the gap between the in-breath and the out-breath. This will enable you to have more control over your breathing, which is very helpful to your overall quality of life.

This must be practiced during activity, not during a meditation sitting. Breathe normally. The important thing is to be attentive to the gap between the in-breath and the out-breath.

Practice this while you are eating. Go on eating, but be attentive to the gap.

Pay attention to the gap between the in- and out-breath while walking. Be fixed at the gap; do not stop the activity.

Throughout any activity you do during the day, pay attention to the gap between the in-breath and out-breath.

LOOKING FOR BEAUTY

When you find yourself in an unpleasant place or circumstance, take a moment to look for the beauty. Every place or circumstance can have some beauty around it. Whether you are in a traffic jam in the summer or in an examination room in a doctor's office, you can find some beauty around you.

Take a deep breath, set aside your feelings of stress and discomfort, and enjoy the beauty. Continue this steady breathing until you feel yourself begin to relax. Savor the beauty.

After a few minutes, shift your focus back to the place or circumstance and note whether your attitude has changed.

Wake-up call: memory

What do you need to let go of or be at peace with? Is there an upsetting memory from your life that still haunts you? Take 20–60 minutes to write the basic storyline and dialogue of this memory. Rewrite the piece and add in what you learned or gained from surviving this event. Then do one last rewrite, this time approaching it as a story that is not personal but as something that others might benefit from. The memory will no longer feel personal and it will be easier to let go of after completing this exercise.

163

Realizing joy

When you are a little down or a little depressed, try this to quiet the mind and body and to realize joy.

Say, "I am breathing in and making the breath-body light and peaceful."

Then say, "I am breathing out and making the breath-body light and peaceful."

"I am breathing in and making my entire body light and peaceful and joyous."

"I am breathing out and making my entire body light and peaceful and joyous."

"I am breathing in while my mind and body are peace and joy."

"I am breathing out while my mind and body are peace and joy."

Try this for 20, 30, or 60 minutes according to your ability and the time available to you.

164

THREE-PART BREATHING II

Lie down with knees bent or in the relaxation pose with your legs separated and flopped open. Have your shoulders and head up a bit higher than the rest of your body.

Take a normal breath in through your nose and then divide your exhalation into three equal parts, out through your mouth or nose, pausing very briefly between each part.

Inhale, exhale-pause, exhale-pause, exhale-pause.

Take 1–2 normal breaths.

Start again.

Inhale, exhale-pause, exhale-pause, exhale-pause.

Take 1–2 normal breaths.

Think of these pauses as if they were little loaves of freshly baked bread, still warm from the oven.

Try to do this exercise for 10 cycles.

165

CYCLE OF LIFE

Sit comfortably and close your eyes. Become aware that trees and
plants are involved in creating the air you breathe.

Animals are breathing the same air.

Other humans are breathing the same air.

This is the cycle of life.

Focus on your breathing and look deeply into this phenomenon
and experience these connections fully. Take slow deep breaths
in through your nose and exhale slowly out your mouth
or nose. Every time you go away from this cycle, let your
breathing bring you back.

Breathe and meditate on this for 10–20 minutes.

Wake-up call: mindfulness

A pebble in your pocket or another item of your choosing
can serve as a teacher—a reminder for when you slip into
automatic pilot and lose awareness. A reminder can teach
you to pause and return to your breathing. Beginning
again is an important part of this practice and is one of
the great muscle builders of mindfulness. It is always okay
to begin again.

166

INSIDE MASSAGE

This is an invitation to massage the inside of your body with your mind.

Sweep your attention through your body like a gentle breeze that moves from the inside out. Breathe normally.

Allow the mind to move unobstructed through the body, especially through areas of discomfort or disease.

Sweep the mind back and forth like a floodlight.

Note the sensations in the body and how they change.

If you lose focus, come back to the breath and then return to this sweeping of the mind through the body.

Shift your awareness into your inner body and take 10–15 minutes to sit and breathe, sensing and feeling the movement of the breath within and around the organs.

167

BELLY EXPANSION

Try a breathing meditation using your abdomen.

Sit and notice how you normally breathe and what parts expand and contract. Notice if you primarily breathe through your nose or mouth. Notice if your stomach expands or stays the same with each breath. Notice if your chest raises or remains level. Become aware of what happens to your body from your normal breathing.

Then start making a conscious effort to expand your belly on the in-breath. Inhale deeply and slowly through your nose into the belly.

Also make a conscious effort to contract on the out-breath. Exhale deeply and slowly and make a conscious effort to contract your belly.

Do this for 20 cycles.

Finish the meditation by breathing naturally. You should experience a more relaxed and rhythmic breathing style.

168

Inner Smile Meditation

Close your eyes, forming a half-smile with your lips, and feel
the smile moving up to your eyes. Relax and begin to breathe
slowly in and out through your nose. Slow the breathing.

When you feel your eyes filled with the energy of your smile, you
can begin to send this energy down through your body.

Smile into your jaw, tongue, neck, throat, heart, internal organs,
etc. Smile into your jaw, tongue, neck, throat, heart, internal
organs, muscles, joints, until you have breathed the smile into
every part of your body.

Put a smile into your swallow so it goes through your digestive system.

Smile from your eyes down to your spine.

Relax and soften.

You can then work your way back up to your eyes to complete the
meditation. This should take about 10 minutes.

First chakra

Sit quietly, close your eyes, and take a few slow deep breaths, relaxing.

Rest your awareness gently on your perineum, which is about halfway between the anus and genitals. Contract the area on the inhalation and relax it on the exhalation.

Imagine a feeling of power surging into this "root" center from the deep center of the earth.

As it increases, keep your attention on this powerful magnetic energy at the bottom of your spine.

Focusing at the base of the spine, imagine that with each breath, energy collects and builds up there.

Continue to relax, and sense the feelings in the coccyx, perineum, anus, and deep inside your pelvic cavity, the foundation of your body.

Sensing your root center, breathe for 10 minutes or more as if the earth's energy is coming directly into you from below. Feel the strength and power of this energy.

170

Pranayamic Walking

Set a destination and simply walk while taking note of your breath. It does not matter how long your walk is.

Deliberately breathe in and out through your nose, even though it may seem more natural or easier through your mouth.

By consciously breathing through your nose, you use your body's natural filtration system.

Now your walk has become a movement meditation.

One of the most important effects of breath awareness techniques is that you regularly observe your breath. Observing your breath allows you to shift your posture and mind toward a balance, a center. As you center your body with an awareness of your breath, you can be more fully in the world.

Whenever you lose focus on your breath during the walk, get back to the breath as quickly as you can. Don't worry about this happening, because it will.

Be fully in this walk you are taking. Enjoy this time and the increased energy you have.

171

SMILING AT YOU

Sit. Relax your eyes and let the sensation of relaxation spread through your whole face.

Now visualize someone you care about smiling at you. Breathe slow, deep inhalations and exhalations.

Let their smile enter you and smile back at them.

Maintain this for several minutes and you will soon find yourself smiling naturally.

If you get away from your breath, don't worry. It will happen a thousand times. Feel happy coming back to the breath. Don't worry that you're going to have to do it a thousand times. That is why this is called practice.

Wake-up call: moderation

Moderation is the only way to find true balance and the best way to live fully and with mindful awareness. Pleasure in moderation relaxes and tempers the spirit. Ralph Waldo Emerson said it best: "Moderation in all things, especially moderation."

172

BREATHING DURING CONVERSATION

While talking with people, you can have more meaningful conversations by following your breath. It is a simple act, but propels you into the present moment of the conversation so you are more aware of what is being said and what you are saying.

Follow your breath while carrying on a conversation by breathing long, light, even breaths through your nose.

Follow your breath while listening to the other person's words and to your own replies. Whether you are listening or talking, continue to follow your breath for the entire conversation. Every time you lose track of the breath, just gently go back to your awareness of it.

Enjoy your conversation in the present moment.

Wake-up call: morality

The essence of morality is represented by the wisdom of not harming others, even with words. The joy you experience when you are practicing morality gives rise to the happiness of concentration and purity of mind. When the mind is steady and one-pointed, there's a quality of inner peace and stillness that is much deeper and more fulfilling than the happiness of sense pleasures.

173

AH

AH is considered the source of all speech and sound, the sound of openness.

Allow the sound AH to come out naturally with your breath. Inhale slowly and deeply through your nose. As you exhale through your mouth, produce the sound AH. Let the sound emit from you as long as your breath allows.

Enjoy this peaceful sound and fill the world with it.

Use AH to remove all feelings of imperfection, all guilt, all negative energies in you. A two-letter sound can create quite a positive feeling within you.

Feel pure, healthy, and strong. Relax in the experience and be one with the sound for 5–10 minutes.

174

Awareness of Thoughts and Spaces

Sit and close your eyes. Relax.

Know you are breathing in. Inhale through your nose.

Know you are breathing out. Exhale through your mouth or nose.

Be aware of a thought as it arises in your mind. Smile to it.

Be aware of the end of a thought as it passes out of your mind.
    Smile to it.

Be aware of the space between the thoughts in your mind.

Be aware that you are not caught up in thinking.

Feel calm and stable. Dwell in the present moment.

Continue this until you reach what feels like full awareness.

NO DOGS
on Beach/Esports
Nov 1 thru Oct 15

175

Breathe away drowsiness

If you feel drowsy, don't go for the coffee or an energy drink, open your eyes and either scan the body or follow the breath.

Begin scanning your external body. Become aware of your limbs, hands, feet, head, and torso.

Then scan your internal body. Become aware of your organs, bones, blood, and cells. During your scan of your body, concentrate on your breathing. Deep and slow inhalations through your nose and steady exhalations through your mouth or nose.

You can count your breaths to help stay present. When you lose count, start over.

If you can practice mindful breathing for 5 minutes, allowing your body to rest, then you can stop the focus on thinking.

If you can stop the focus on thinking and believing your thinking, you increase the quality of your being. There is more peace, relaxation, and rest. You will no longer feel drowsy.

176

DAILY AWARENESS

It is important that you learn to practice full awareness of breathing in your daily life.

You can begin to enter the present moment by becoming aware of your breath.

Breathing in and out, you can smile to affirm you are in control of yourself.

Through awareness of breathing, you can be awake in, and to, the present moment.

Full awareness of your breathing helps your mind stop wandering in confused, never-ending thoughts.

Do this for 5 minutes several different times per day.

177

BODY SCAN MEDITATION

Lie on your back with your legs uncrossed, your arms at your sides, palms up, and your eyes open or closed, in the relaxation pose.

Focus on your breathing, how the air moves in and out of your body. Slowly and deeply breathe in through your nose and out through your mouth or nose.

After several slow, deep breaths, as you begin to feel comfortable and relaxed, direct your attention to the toes of your left foot.

Tune into any sensations in that part of your body while remaining aware of your breathing. It often helps to imagine each breath flowing to the spot where you are directing your attention. Focus on your left toes for 1–2 minutes.

Then move your focus to the sole of your left foot and hold it there for a minute or two while continuing to pay attention to your breathing.

Follow the same procedure as you move to your left ankle, calf, knee, thigh, hip, and so on all around the body. Then move to the right side of your body beginning, again, with your right toes, and continue until you have gone all around the body.

Pay particular attention to the head: the jaw, chin, lips, tongue, roof of the mouth, nostrils, throat, cheeks, eyelids, eyes, eyebrows, forehead, temples, and scalp.

Finally, focus on the very top of your hair, the uppermost part of your body.

The body scan meditation can take a while, 10–20 minutes.

Then let go of the body altogether, and in your mind, hover above yourself as your breath reaches beyond you and touches the universe. Savor this breath because it is precious.

Wake-up call: motivation

It is important to be mindful of what you are doing when you speak, of what the motivation is behind what you are saying. However, we usually act out of habit and do not realize what our underlying motivations are. The more you can get in touch with your motivations, the more likely it is that you will say things in ways that are in harmony with your deepest values.

178

Expanding breath

Exhale all of your breath through your nose or mouth by sucking in your stomach muscles.

Use your right thumb to close your right nostril and slowly inhale through the left nostril.

Fill your lungs to a comfortable capacity and close your left nostril with whatever finger feels most natural to you. Keep holding your breath for as long as possible, but don't overdo it. Be aware of your limits.

Then open the right nostril while keeping the left side closed and slowly exhale through the left nostril.

Again, exhale all of your breath through your nose by sucking in your stomach muscles.

This time, use your left thumb to close your left nostril and slowly inhale through the right nostril.

Fill your lungs to a comfortable capacity and close your right nostril with whatever finger feels most natural to you. Keep holding your breath for as long as possible.

Repeat the cycle five times at each session, gradually increasing the number to 12 times.

179

SHOPPING AND BREATHING

Going shopping at a store, whether for groceries or clothes or
anything else, is a good time to become aware of your breath. It
will help you become a mindful shopper.

When you begin shopping, pause before the entrance to the store
and take 3 mindful breaths to calm and orient yourself before
you walk in. Inhale through your nose and exhale through
your mouth.

Allow your body to relax before you begin and see if a smile is
possible. Continue your shopping in a mindful way.

When you check out or leave a store, breathe deeply and stay in
the present moment. Did your shopping change because you
were more awake and aware?

Wake-up call: music

You enjoy sense pleasures, like listening to music, but at
a certain point you tire of them. Just how long can you
listen to music and have it still be pleasant? By contrast,
the happiness that comes with concentration of mind is
refreshing. It energizes you. When nothing is yearned for,
you are free to enjoy what you do, free to hear the music
in all things.

180

Time-out

Take a mindful time-out, whether it is a coffee break, visit to
the bathroom or water cooler, or a short walk down the hall.
Whatever time-out you take, focus on your breathing.

Pay attention to the surroundings. Continue your steady breathing.

Smile. Complete your time-out and continue to smile.

Wake-up call: non-doing

Meditation is non-doing. It does not involve trying to
get something else done or get somewhere else. It
emphasizes doing what you are doing and being where
you already are. The more complicated the world gets
and the more intrusive it becomes on your personal
psychological space and privacy, the more important it
will be to practice non-doing.

181

Counting backward

Meditate by counting backward from 100. Begin with a few slow, deep breaths. Inhale and exhale through your nose. Let your nose act as a filter for the incoming air.

Visualize rowing a boat toward an island and with each pull of the oars, feel the movements and your breath become slower and longer and more relaxed.

At zero, you arrive on the island and can continue with a silent meditation. Your breathing will automatically be relaxed and steady.

Wake-up call: non-harming

No one who truly loves herself could harm another, for she would be harming herself. The essence of morality and virtue is represented by the wisdom of not harming others, even with words.

182

Forward bend

Stand with your feet hip-width apart, knees fluidly bent, and bend your torso forward over the thighs. Take a few deep breaths in through your nose and out through your nose or mouth. Relax.

On an inhalation, allow the weight of your breath to drop the torso so the spinal column elongates. On an exhalation, let your shoulder blades release.

A natural oscillation of the whole body will occur, releasing deeply held tensions. This exercise is soothing and comforting.

Passively witness the sensations associated with the in-breath and the out-breath.

By focusing your attention and breathing action you will have the feeling of being more grounded.

Use the forward bend for as long as you feel comfortable. It is calming, but also rejuvenating.

183

Dealing with life

Sit with your arms extended straight in front of you, slightly below shoulder level and parallel to the ground.

Close your right hand into a fist.

Wrap your left hand around the right so the fingers of the left hand are over the knuckles of the right fist. The heels of the hands touch.

Straighten the thumbs, extending them up so that the sides are touching.

Focus your eyes so that you gaze at the thumbs.

Inhale for 5 seconds, exhale for 5 seconds, hold the breath for 15 seconds.

Start with 3–5 minutes of this, working up to 11 minutes.

This centering exercise can help you deal with difficult situations, which come up more often than we like.

184

SOLIDIFYING THE BREATH

Sit and breathe normally for a few rounds.

Make a fist with each of your hands, closing your fingers loosely over your thumbs.

Then squeeze your thumbs firmly with steady pressure and hold for a minute. As soon as you squeeze your thumbs, your breathing will become markedly deeper and stronger. The harder you squeeze your thumbs, the deeper your breathing will become and the stronger you will feel.

Your mind will feel calmer.

After another minute, release your thumbs and allow your breathing to return to its original state.

This exercise can evolve by squeezing your thumbs even harder and holding for more time.

Doing this will deepen and strengthen your breathing and groundedness.

FOCUS ON EXHALING

You can work with anxiety by focusing on your exhalations and lengthening them, deliberately and gradually. By focusing on your exhalations you are releasing the anxiety you are feeling and replacing it with calmness.

Begin by breathing normally. Count how long your exhalation lasts.

If your everyday exhalation lasts 6 counts, draw each one out to seven for a few breathing cycles, then to eight for a few cycles, and so on, until you find a length that suits you.

Do this exercise for at least 10 cycles.

Wake-up call: non-judging

A judging mind is filled with constant nagging prattle, a voice of internal dialogue that supports ego—all the yes/nos, good/bads, right/wrongs contribute to judging the mind's power. When judging arises, if you acknowledge it with spacious, non-judgmental attention, you loosen its grasp. If you are simply aware that the mind is judging when it is judging and acknowledge it with open, clear attention, the judging mind begins to dissolve.

186

Raised pulse

When you sense that your pulse or heartbeat is increasing, call a time-out. Take a few minutes to try to regain control.

During a time-out, begin by taking slow, deep breaths in through your nose and out through your mouth. While you continue your breathing, try to think of other ways to help you calm down.

Replace thoughts that reinforce distress and arousal with distress-reducing thoughts.

When you feel your pulse or heartbeat begin to go back to normal because you are in control of it, release yourself from your time-out.

Wake-up call: nutrition

Practice mindful food consumption. Vow to ingest only items that preserve peace, well-being, and joy in your body and in your consciousness. The Buddha advised us to identify the kinds of nutriments that have been feeding our pain and then simply to stop ingesting them. The moment you resolve to stop feeding your suffering, a path appears in front of you. You can apply this practice to other things you ingest through other senses.

Six healing exhalations

The Six Healing Exhalations is an ancient breathing practice of
Taoism. This simple exercise can be done in any posture and is
a great way to become more energized.

The pronunciation, sound, and order of this exercise have
variations. I feel this example is a very good one to use.

One should take a deep breath in through the nose and let it out
slowly through the mouth. Let the nose be a cleansing filter for
the incoming air.

There is one way of drawing breath in and six ways of expelling
breath out: SSSS (lung sound), WOOO (kidney sound),
SHHHH (liver sound), HAAA (heart sound), WHOOO
(spleen sound), HEEE (balancing of energies sound):

SSSS
WOOO
SHHHH
HAAA
WHOOO
HEEE

You make the 6 sounds, 3 times each.

There are a number of variations for the sounds, found in books
and online, but all are for better health and reduced stress.

188

Breathe away anger

When you feel yourself getting angry, breathe for at least 10
counts. You have heard this advice often in life: count to 10.

When you feel yourself getting angry, take a long, deep inhalation,
through your nose, and, as you do, say the number 1
to yourself.

Then, relax your entire body as you breathe out.

Repeat the same process with number 2, all the way through *at
least* 10 (if you're really angry, continue to 25).

What you are doing here is clearing your mind with a mini version
of a meditation exercise. The combination of counting and
breathing is so relaxing that it's almost impossible to remain
angry once you are finished.

The increased oxygen in your lungs and the time gap between
the moment you became angry and the time you finished the
exercise enables you to increase your perspective.

The exercise is equally effective in working with stress or
frustration. Whenever you feel a little off, give it a try. The truth
is, this exercise is a wonderful way to spend a minute or two
whether or not you're angry.

189

Sun breath

Do a sun breath practice before meditation or sleep.

Stand in the mountain pose, erect as if a string is pulling you up from the scalp, with your hands by your sides. Breathe into your belly, through your nose, while stretching your arms.

Release your breath.

Breathe in and bring your hands to namaste, prayer position, at your heart.

Stretch your hands out and exhale, then inhale, lifting your hands over your head.

Exhale and lower your hands to your sides.

Do this 9 times.

To breathe fully is to live fully, to manifest the full range and power of your inborn potential for vitality in everything that you sense, feel, think, and do.

Relaxation with head touching a wall

For 3 minutes, practice the relaxation pose with the top of your head touching a wall. You melt into the floor, legs splayed, arms slightly away from the body with palms up.

Observe your natural breath and relax your neck. Breathe in and out until your breathing is controlled and your neck is relaxed.

Then, for 5 minutes, bring your attention to the entrance of your nostrils and upper lip.

Then come back to breathing naturally.

Your head touching the wall gives you a different experience and keeps you from falling asleep in the relaxation pose.

Wake-up call: observation

Things can be a certain way without needing to be acted upon or judged or even pushed aside. They can simply be observed. In observing thoughts, it is important not to comment on or judge their content, but see them as they arise. And by observing the intention that precedes voluntary activity, like walking, you gain more freedom because you become aware of how little you can control.

191

Exactly as it is

Try stopping, sitting down, and becoming aware of your breathing
once in a while throughout the day. It can be for 5 minutes
or 5 seconds. Time is not the important thing here. What is
important is the act of becoming aware of your breathing.

Let go into full acceptance of the present moment, including what
you are feeling and what you perceive to be happening. Do not
try to change anything at all.

Just breathe and let go. Breathe and let be.

You do not need anything to be different in this moment. Give
yourself permission to allow this moment to be exactly as it is,
and allow yourself to be exactly as you are. Continue your long,
slow deep breaths.

When you are ready, after 5 minutes or more, move in the direction
your heart tells you to go, mindfully and with resolution.

192

BATHTIME

Allow 30–45 minutes for taking a bath.

Do not hurry. Let every movement be slow.

Pay attention. Be aware of every part of your body. Be aware of the water. Remember over 95 percent of your life is spent outside of water. While your body is in the water, enjoy the sensation of having your skin touching the water.

Follow your breath. Breathe in and out through your nose.

When you finish, your mind and body should feel light, peaceful, and clean.

As you towel off to dry, take one last slow deep breath in and out through your nose and send loving kindness to everyone, including yourself.

Wake-up call: openness

Learn a natural openness of heart. Develop a non-grasping openness to whatever comes next, a calm willingness to be present. Have an ease and openness of mind that receives with interest every kind of circumstances—asking what you can learn from each experience.

BREATHING FOR ALERTNESS

Poor breathing robs energy and negatively affects mental alertness. Many people who do not practice healthy breathing suffer lack of energy and alertness. The electrical quality of the air you breathe also has an effect on serotonin levels and thus creative alertness. The amount of serotonin we have is believed to have an impact on our feelings of well-being and happiness.

Inhale through your nostrils for 6 counts, hold for 4, exhale through your mouth for 2, hold for 2.

When breathing in, be alert to everything in that moment. When breathing out, be alert to the moment in all its totality. Being aware of the breath: that is alertness and increases your energy level.

Wake-up call: patience

Frustrations with people or situations are occasions to practice patience. Do you have the patience to wait until the mind settles before you act? The power of patience is seen in the effect of many drops of water onto a rock over time.

CLEANSING BREATH II

Deep breathing multiplies the pace in which the body eliminates toxins. Deep breathing and exercise can accelerate this cleansing process by as much as 15 times the normal pace.

To cleanse your body through effective breathing, remember the formula 1-4-2:

1 = number of counts while inhaling
4 = number of counts to hold your breath
2 = number of counts while exhaling

Breathe in through the nose for a slow count of 1, hold for 4 counts, and breathe out through the nose for a slow count of 4.

Use the numbers that are most comfortable for you. You can substitute numbers as long as they are multiples of the basic formula, for example, 8-32-16. Breathe in through the nose for a slow count of 8, hold for 32 counts, and breathe out through the nose for a slow count of 16.

Continue for several minutes, with no pause after the exhale.

Make sure to breathe deep into the abdomen, like a vacuum. This helps the lymph system, as when you hold your breath your body can fully oxygenate the blood and activate your lymph system, and as you slowly exhale your body eliminates the toxins through your lymph system.

195

FOOTSTEPS

Walk very slowly, silently, with the eyes lowered, looking toward
the ground.

Mindfulness is maintained while walking, taking one step with
the left foot while breathing in, and one step with the right foot
while breathing out. Let your nose be a filter for the air coming
into your body.

Be aware of all parts of your body while you are walking
and breathing.

When you reach the turnaround point, pause, becoming aware
of standing. Then slowly walk again using the same technique.
Walk and breathe this way for 10–20 minutes.

Wake-up call: peace

Make a habit of asking yourself, "Is this task or behavior
really necessary or is it just a way to be busy?" If you
can reduce or eliminate some activities, you will achieve
greater peace in your life because you will have slowed
things down.

196

LONG COUNT BREATHS

Long count breathing is a great way to get focused in the morning before your workday begins or to energize yourself midday. When doing the long count breathing, inhale and exhale through your nostrils.

Take a long breath and when the lungs are full, mentally count "one."

Breathe out completely until the lungs are empty, mentally count "two."

Take a long breath again and count "three" and breathe out "four."

Do this up to ten, then backward from ten to one, back and forth.

Wake-up call: perception

The problem is often in your own perception. Save everyone grief by waiting a little while to see if your perception changes. Perception can be wildly different from the facts in many cases. You control how you perceive things in your mind. When you are confident that your perception is accurate, then move on. You will learn that whether you regard any situation as good or bad depends on your perception.

197

Mantra so hum

This contemplation exercise uses the mantra "so hum," which is
not only a reflection of the sound of the breath but also carries a
contemplative meaning: "I am that" (*so* = "I am" and *hum* = "that").
Here, "that" refers to all of creation, the one breathing us all.

Find a comfortable seated position. Relax any bodily tension.
Focus on your breath.

As you inhale through your mouth, silently say "so" to yourself
and as you exhale, again, through your mouth, say "hum."

Once the "so hum" rhythm has been established, begin to
contemplate the meaning of "so hum."

As you inhale with the mantra "so," say to yourself " I am,"
connecting to your essential self.

As you exhale with "hum," inwardly say "that" or "all that is."

Feel how your exhalation releases you into the expanse around
you, back into "all that is." Stay with this contemplation until
you naturally begin to settle.

If a thought arises, come back to the simple mantra, "so hum."

Do this for 10, 20, or 30 minutes.

198

AWARENESS OF PAIN

If there is a place in your body that is sick or in pain, take this time to become aware of it and send it your love.

Breathing in, allow the sick or pained area to rest, and breathing out, smile to it with great tenderness and affection.

Be aware that there are other parts of your body that are still strong and healthy. Allow these strong areas to send their strength and energy to the weak or sick area. This will happen with each inhalation and exhalation.

Breathe in and affirm your own capacity to heal, breathe out and let go of the worry or fear you may be holding.

Do this exercise for 10–20 minutes.

SIPPING BREATH

Observe your natural breath with your eyes closed.

Once your natural breath is steady, place your tongue against the upper palate of your mouth and slowly breathe in through your mouth. This will cause a sipping sound.

At the end of the in-breath, relax your tongue, close your mouth, and hold the breath in your lungs for as long as comfortable.

Then release it through your nose. Feel the inspiration that fills your mind and body. You are now stronger than you were before you started this exercise.

Do this for 5–10 repetitions.

Wake-up call: perspective

How often do you let yourself be affected by the behavior of others so dramatically that you do things you wouldn't do if you had maintained a clearer perspective? Mindfulness dramatically amplifies the probability that any activity in which you are engaged will result in an expansion of your perspective, of who you are. It's a remembering, a reminding yourself to be awake and aware.

200

Reaction to thinking

We create much suffering in our lives by reacting to our thoughts. When we are able to accept these thoughts and stop reacting to them, we eliminate a lot of that suffering.

Begin by sitting comfortably in a chair or on a cushion and take a few deep breaths, focusing on the in-breath and out-breath.

Note your thoughts and feelings when they arise but especially note any move to avoid or push away what you do not like.

Welcome these thoughts and accept them.

You will get a feel for accepting and letting go. That is the key, to accept and then let go. Over and over again. Do this exercise for 5–10 minutes.

Wake-up call: practice

The practices of mindfulness and loving-kindness help us to understand that all things deserve care. When you relate to all things with mindfulness and loving-kindness, you are relating to yourself with mindfulness and loving-kindness.

201

Conscious Slump

Everyone who sits at a desk for any length of time could use a pick-me-up, a way to reenergize.

At your desk, do a conscious slump. Let your spine curl forward and your head drop slowly.

Feel the weight of your shoulders as they slump forward. Relax.

Stay with the gentle stretch and breathe. Concentrate on a slow, steady breath in and out.

You are allowing your upper body to give in to gravity.

Then, slowly, sit erect. Move your body up and continue to concentrate on your breathing.

Savor the body sensations you have. The exercise can be done for 5 minutes or more.

You can do this exercise as many times as you like at your desk throughout the day. It is better than getting a cup of coffee or energy drink. It is also a good exercise to do at the beginning and end of every meditation.

2O2

Spinal Breathing

Sit comfortably in a chair or on a cushion with back support and close your eyes. Breathe naturally in and out through the nose until you feel yourself relax.

Then slow down your breathing and make each breath deeper, expelling more air than in normal breathing.

Now imagine a tiny nerve, like a little ribbon or thread running from your tailbone all the way up to the center of your forehead, the third eye. The tiny nerve that goes between these two is the spinal nerve.

In spinal breathing, you trace the spinal nerve with your attention as you breathe. You go up from the root to the brow on inhalation and down from the brow to the root on exhalation.

If your mind wanders, bring it back to this practice and reengage with spinal breathing.

Try to do this twice a day, starting with 5 minutes.

203

Breath at the Nostrils

There are many teachings that say that while you breathe you should be aware of your nostrils, the place where air enters and leaves the body.

This is likened to looking at the place where the saw touches the log, the hammer touches the nail. It is the power point, the point of impact.

Get yourself in a comfortable position either sitting or standing. Allowing the body to just breathe naturally, bring the attention to the most noticeable point of touch where the breath makes contact as it enters the nostrils.

Bring the awareness to the sense of touch of the air as it passes in and passes out. Keep your attention at one precise point and note the sensation that accompanies each breath as it flows in and flows out of the body in the natural breathing process.

If the attention strays, bring it back to the point where you notice the breath as it comes and at the nostrils, noting "breathing in; breathing out." Not thinking about the breath. Not even visualizing it. Just being with the sensation as it arises with the touch of the air passing in and out of the nostrils.

Do this exercise for 5–10 minutes.

204

SMILING AT OTHERS

An easy and effective way to make the world a better place is to simply smile at people you see, acquaintances and strangers alike.

Begin by concentrating on your breath. This enables you to get in control of your mind and body. Smile at the people you see. You can start by looking at them directly in the eyes and acknowledging them as fellow human beings. Then relax the mouth area and smile. A nice, bright smile like the sun coming up on a beautiful day.

When you smile at friends and strangers, an interesting phenomenon occurs—you smile away your irritation and anger. You achieve a victory for yourself and humanity. The world becomes a better place because of this simple act.

Wake-up call: present moment

There is a layer of "concept" that sits between you and the reality of the present moment. To touch the present moment, you have to let that layer of concept drop away. To do this, you first have to be able to stop or pause. You have to stop both body and mind. When your mind stops racing, when you allow yourself to be in one place, you can be truly present in the here and now.

205

RETENTION BREATH

If you need a quick fix to reduce stress and anxiety in your life, then this retention breath exercise will help you do the trick. One of the benefits of this breathing exercise is that it quickly decreases stress and anxiety in your mind and body.

Sit and breathe in through the nose slowly and calmly. Relax.

At the top of the inhale, hold the breath gently. Feel the retained energy circulating and radiating in the body.

When it is time to exhale, release the breath calmly and slowly through the mouth and then pause, waiting patiently for the next inhale.

Continue for several minutes. You can also do this and focus the held energy into a specific part of the body to help relax it or heal it. Do this exercise for 3–5 minutes.

206

Aswini mudra

Lie on your back with your knees bent and feet on the floor.
Breathe rhythmically for about 20–30 seconds. Relax your body.

Pull the sphincter (opening of the rectum) and all the pelvic floor
muscles inward and upward. Hold the tension for a count of 3,
breathing rhythmically while you do so, and relax.

Practice this mudra for up to 30 seconds.

Repeat 6 times. Then relax.

Wake-up call: reading

Read slowly and calmly so that the very act of reading
is peace. When you are reading, try stopping every half
hour. Close your eyes for a minute or so and bring your
attention back to your breath. Become more aware of
the room and the noises or the silence. This will help you
concentrate better when you begin to read again so you
do not have to constantly reread paragraphs.

207

RELAX

Sit comfortably in a chair or on a cushion and bring your attention to your breathing, which should be natural.

When you feel ready, repeat the word RELAX to yourself, either silently or out loud.

Say the first syllable RE as you breathe in and second syllable LAX as you breathe out.

Do not try to force your breathing into a rhythm or pattern, just keep breathing normally and match the speed of the syllables RE and LAX to the breathing.

When your mind wanders, just bring it back gently and continue to repeat the word RELAX.

Repeat for 5–10 minutes or for as long as this feels comfortable.

208

SQUARE BREATHING

Square breathing is a good stress relief breathing exercise.

Sit comfortably in a chair or on a cushion and close your eyes.
Feel your body begin to relax.

Inhale slowly through your nose for a count of 4, hold for 4, pause
for 4, exhale slowly through the mouth for 4.

Repeat this 2–3 times.

Alternatively, you can inhale through your nose for 4, hold for 4,
exhale through the mouth for 4, hold for 4 counts.

The process of breathing, if you can begin to understand it in
relation to the whole of life, shows you the way to let go of the
old and open to the new.

Relaxed exhales

Slowing and regularizing the breath aids the parasympathetic nervous system, a complex biological mechanism that calms and soothes us.

In stressful times, we typically breathe too rapidly. This leads to a buildup of oxygen in the bloodstream and a corresponding decrease in the relative amount of carbon dioxide, which in turn upsets the ideal acid-alkaline balance (the pH level) of the blood.

In contrast, slowing the breath raises the carbon dioxide level in the blood, which nudges the pH level back to a less alkaline state. As the blood's pH changes, the parasympathetic nervous system calms us in a variety of ways, including telling the vagus nerve to secrete acetylcholine, a substance that lowers the heart rate.

Find a comfortable position to sit in. Focus your awareness on your breath.

Take a long, deep breath in through your nose. Then try long, relaxed exhales and hold the breath on the bottom of each exhale.

Once you've comfortably increased the length of your exhalations by a few counts, turn part of your attention to the subtle sound of them. You'll notice that each one makes a soft HA, like a gentle sigh.

Try to make this sound (and your exhalations) as soft and even as possible from beginning to end.

Hold the breath briefly at the end/bottom of each exhalation, resting peacefully in the stillness.

Continuing like this, watch your breath as steadily as you can for 10–15 minutes.

Wake-up call: relaxation

Happiness cannot be found through great effort and willpower. Cultivating mindfulness teaches us to calm down enough to enter and dwell in states of deep relaxation. Watching television (for example) hardly ever promotes physiological or psychological relaxation, but taking a walk through a natural area does.

Wake-up call: respect

To say you love someone is not enough; you also need to be respectful of them. Love produces lasting happiness and that comes from a deep respect for all beings and all life. This helps you connect with others and nature by a feeling of respect rather than by fear. It is almost impossible to love something you fear.

210

Exhale out a mood

Whenever you feel your mind is not tranquil, exhale deeply, as much as you can, throwing the air out of you, either through your nose or mouth.

The mood will be thrown out, too!

Expel the breath as far as possible.

Then pull the belly in and retain for a few seconds without inhaling.

Then allow the body to inhale deeply.

Stop then for 3 seconds.

Repeat, making this exercise a rhythm.

You will feel a change coming into your whole being. The mood will go.

211

RELAXATION WITH CHAIR

When you feel the need to relax your body and mind, find a chair and lie on the floor with your calves supported on the chair.

With your legs higher than your belly, you will feel the completion of exhalations more strongly.

For 5 minutes, inhale and exhale smoothly, without effort.

Then bring your awareness to the silence at the bottom of your exhalations, feeling them fade into emptiness.

Pause intentionally for 1–2 seconds at the bottom of each exhalation.

Return to the relaxation pose on the ground for 2 minutes before ending the exercise.

Wake-up call: restraint

With wisdom and awareness, you can see that there are skillful activities that are conducive to greater happiness and understanding—and there are unskillful ones that lead to further suffering and conflict. Restraint is the capacity you have to discriminate one from the other. Find the strength and composure of mind to pursue the skillful course.

212

DEALING WITH IMPATIENCE

It is good to examine impatience when it arises. You want to adopt
the perspective that sees things as unfolding in their own time.
It helps to listen to the moment, breathe, let things be as they
are, let go into patience.

Choose the longest line at the grocery store, the bank,
the tollbooth.

Listening, even when you feel pressure or blockage, will guide
you. Wait patiently and listen.

Breathe slowly and focus on your impatience. See the impatience
leave you with each exhale. In its place will be calmness.

Wake-up call: reverence

Become aware of any living beings in your world (people,
animals, plants) who you ignore or take for granted
and cultivate a sense of reverence for them. This deep
respect is important. When you have a deep respect for
others, then you also have a deep respect for yourself.

213

Soft vision

Walk with "soft vision," allowing the eyes to relax and focus upon nothing, while aware of everything. It may seem difficult to do at first. With practice, you will be able to control it like flicking on and off a switch. It is all a matter of concentrating on nothing but also being aware of everything.

Once you have discovered your natural rhythm, lock into it, so that the rhythm of the walking sets the rhythm for the breath like a metronome.

In order to connect more deeply with all the healing elements within and around you, you may want to stop walking from time to time and simply breathe.

The more you make yourself available to these elements, the more you are refreshed and healed. Try to stay with this exercise for 5–20 minutes.

214

At the computer

Sometimes it feels like we are always connected to a computer, laptop, tablet, or smartphone.

When you need to refocus and feel human again, take 3 mindful breaths before turning on your computer, opening your laptop, checking your messages.

At your computer, pause every now and then to follow your breathing and notice how you are sitting.

If you are a bit tense, stretch your neck different ways, straighten your spine, and relax your body. Take long, deep inhalations and exhalations.

During gaps in the flow of your work, come back to your breathing.

You can also do a forward bend while sitting or standing, and this can be very rejuvenating.

Stop, sit, breathe. Listen, look, feel, smell. You deserve a break!

215

BASE CHAKRA

Sit and breathe in and out through your nose.

Imagine that you are drawing air in through the base chakra, located between the anus and genitals.

As you draw breath in, imagine that it flows upward until it reaches your heart.

As you breathe out, visualize the air flowing down to join the air of the next in-breath.

You will become aware that you are breathing deeply and low. You may feel warmth or coolness in the chakra.

Be aware of the feeling of inner energy flowing upward as it completes the circle on the out-breath to return into the body.

Do this exercise for 10–15 minutes.

216

Cat–Cow Stretch

The cat-cow stretch is perfect in the morning and evening and whenever your back can use a good stretch. It is a great warm-up for the spine and helps relax the muscles that go tense from too much sitting.

Come to all fours.

Draw your tailbone down and gently arch the back like a cat, while exhaling.

Then, inhaling, raise the head and tailbone in the air like a cow in a gentle arch.

Go back and forth, synchronizing breath with movement.

Repeat for 10 rounds.

217

Holding your breath

Sit with your eyes closed.

Inhale deeply through the nose, filling the lungs.

Hold the breath for as long as possible.

Then exhale gently through the mouth and keep the lungs empty
for as long as possible.

Continue this breathing for 10 minutes.

Return to normal breathing and just being still.

Then, with your eyes closed, stand up and let your body be loose
and receptive. The subtle energies will be felt to move the body.
Allow this to happen for 10 minutes.

Then lie down with your eyes closed, silent and still, for 10 minutes.

218

Taking care of discomfort

Know you are breathing in. Know you are breathing out. Be aware of your whole body.

Smile to your body. Be aware of a place in your body where you have pain or discomfort. Welcome it and smile to it with compassion.

Be aware of the pain or discomfort as it changes, getting stronger or weaker.

Be aware of the feeling that lies at the heart of the pain or discomfort. Dwell in the present moment.

Breathing and receiving what you need, releasing old limitations, resting in wholeness, tune into the positive healing qualities you need at this time.

Do this exercise for around 10–20 minutes.

219

Breathing Spaces

Put your attention on the movement of air through your nose during inhalation.

Take several long, slow breaths.

Feel the empty spacious quality of the air as it moves down through your airway to the lungs.

Sense this spaciousness moving down through the tissues and organs of your abdomen, filling your lower breathing space, from the navel down.

This can also be done with the middle breathing space, from the diaphragm to the navel, and upper breathing space, the head to the diaphragm.

Allow any tensions and stagnant energies to release. As you exhale slowly, direct these out with the breath. Keep working with these spaces for 10 minutes.

220

FLUSHING BREATH

Flush out your whole body and mind with this exercise.

Sit comfortably with your eyes closed.

Inhale for 2 counts, with the lowest part of the lungs filled and abdomen expanding outward.

Hold for 2 counts with the lower rib cage expanding.

Exhale for 6 counts with the chest beginning to expand.

Hold for 4 counts. The top of the chest is filled with breath and the throat and shoulders are feeling expanded.

Continue with this exercise for 5–10 minutes.

Wake-up call: ritual

Try thinking about something as a ritual, which has a positive transforming effect on the activity. It is healthy to leave time for these small, sacred rituals in your life. For example, as you approach your morning shower, reflect upon the many sacred rituals involving water. Be aware in the shower. Completely immerse yourself in this experience. Let all ills, transgressions, and preoccupations be washed away.

221

Inhaling OM

Begin by going for a walk, preferably alone and outside.

Inhale, silently saying OM to the count of 2.

Mentally see that the oxygen coming into your body is filled with life-force energy and hold the breath in your mouth.

As you force the air against your cheeks, let them fill to capacity and bulge out. Keep pressing the air into your cheeks as long as you can, without creating discomfort.

Then exhale to the count of 7.

Feel how your concentration has increased and how much more you are noticing on your walk.

Repeat this 12 times or for your entire walk if you wish.

222

Dropping deeply

For 5 minutes, practice the relaxation pose. Lie comfortably on your back on the floor or bed, legs apart with feet flopped open, arms slightly away from your sides with your palms up.

Inhale through your nose, filling your throat, chest, and abdomen.

On the exhale, through your mouth or nose, drop deeply into the surface. You are melting into the surface and there is no observation or consciousness.

Relax your eyes and the skin on your face and continue the relaxation on your exhalations.

Do this for at least 10 minutes.

Wake-up call: savoring

By learning how to be, how to wake up, how to live in the now, you learn how to savor every drop of life. You may find you don't want to waste time distractedly stuffing food down yourself or staring at a really bad TV show (or all the other things you can distract yourself with), but that you want to savor this time and lead the fullest and most rewarding life that you can.

223

THOUGHT, BREATH

Sit comfortably on a cushion or in a chair, erect as if a string was
   pulling you up. This is a meditation posture.

The idea here is to notice whatever enters your mind without
   judging, clinging, or pushing it away. Then return to the breath.

Notice the thought, return to the breath.

Notice the thought, return to the breath.

Notice the thought, return to the breath.

Notice the thought, return to the breath.

Notice the thought, return to the breath.

Notice the thought, return to the breath.

Notice the thought, return to the breath.

Notice the thought, return to the breath.

Notice the thought, return to the breath.

Notice the thought, return to the breath.

After you have done this 10 times, remain seated and follow your breathing. If you found the exercise helpful, go back to doing it as long as you have time for this practice.

Wake-up call: selflessness

An ethically responsible life is one of the most reliable paths to contentment. Thoughtful good intentions, combined with selfless, courageous action, are the cornerstones of contentment and a happy life. Small acts of selflessness provide you with good practice and the building blocks for a compassionate life. Try this: let others take what they need first, share anything you are given if at all possible, and let others decide how you will jointly spend your leisure time.

Wake-up call: sensitivity

Meditation is waking up, becoming acutely sensitive, knowing, feeling, living in the present moment in its pristine state. Breathe in, sensitive to everything, and breathe out, sensitive to everything. After meditation, choose any action in your day that is taken for granted. Bring to that activity the clear intention to attend closely to all its details. Listen to your body, be sensitive to the quality of your mind. Be wholeheartedly there.

224

STANDING PRANAYAMA

While standing, loosen your neck in a circular motion, increasing blood flow to your hands and arms by moving them around, and also rotating your upper body from your hips.

Then close your eyes, hands on hips, and take some deep breaths.

Deliberately straighten your spine, then take a deep breath into the nose and lean backward from the base of your spine, the rear of your head aiming for your upper back.

Relax for a few moments.

Releasing the breath, move back to a standing position.

Then breathe normally for a few cycles.

Start again, going through the process up to 5 times. Feel how straight and tall your body feels. Not only will your body feel stronger, but your mind will as well.

225

CIRCLE OF BREATH

Circular breathing is a technique used by players of some
wind instruments to produce a continuous tone without
interruption. This is accomplished by breathing *in* through the
nose while simultaneously pushing air *out* through the mouth
using air stored in the cheeks.

Sit and breathe in a continuous flow, without interruption
or pause.

You need to be careful with this exercise and do it only for a short
period of time.

The inhale leads directly to the exhale, without stopping or
holding the breath in, and vice versa.

Puff the cheeks and breath normally with the cheeks out. Picture a
trumpet player, like Louis Armstrong, with his cheeks puffed out.

Then puff the cheeks and create a small aperture in the lips,
letting air escape through the lips while inhaling and exhaling
normally through the nose. By controlling the muscles in the
cheeks, try to maintain an air stream for 3–5 seconds.

While the air is being forced from the cheeks, inhale quickly and
deeply through the nose.

While the cheeks are still slightly puffed, begin to exhale through the mouth.

As the lungs begin to empty, puff the cheeks, inhale quickly and deeply through the nose.

After a small amount of air has been inhaled, close the soft palate and "switch back" to air used from the lungs.

Repeat several times. You create the image of a moving circle of breath and energy. This is a great breathing exercise to decrease a person's snoring because the lungs are strengthened.

Wake-up call: service

Consciously or unconsciously, every one of us does render some service or other. Being an attentive parent is a great example of this. If you cultivate the habit of doing the service deliberately, your desire for service will steadily grow stronger, and will make you happy while spreading happiness to the world.

Wake-up call: sight

Experience all things with the enthusiasm of a child, as if you were seeing it for the first time. Seeing requires no effort because your nature is seeing. Practice seeing each thing like it is new.

226

Breathing with Your Belly

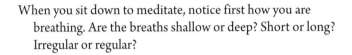

When you sit down to meditate, notice first how you are breathing. Are the breaths shallow or deep? Short or long? Irregular or regular?

As you start this exercise, make a conscious effort to expand your belly when you breathe.

Breathe deeply and slowly into your belly.

Continue breathing this way for 5 minutes.

Then return to breathing naturally. Practice this regularly.

Wake-up call: silence

Think about what it means to take a vow of silence for a short period of time—like one day or even a half day. This is a personal time of rest. Consider an outer and inner silence that is not broken by the continual static of talk, mental chatter, and interpersonal dynamics. You would commune only with yourself and ask only of yourself. Silence is the threshold to the inner sanctum. Silence is the song of the heart.

227

Relaxation, arms above head

Lie down on your back with your legs separated. For 5 minutes, practice the relaxation pose with your arms above your head, loosely holding your elbows.

With a smooth, slightly extended inhalation, feel how your breath naturally moves into your upper chest.

After 2–3 minutes, reverse the cross of your arms so the other forearm is on top.

When you complete this exercise, your mind and body will be relaxed and you may want to do a seated meditation.

Wake-up call: simplicity

Simplicity brings more happiness than complexity. Realize the joy of living a simple life by being unencumbered by unnecessary possessions and incessant desires.

228

Question and answer

First, sit comfortably on a cushion or in a chair. Know you are
   breathing in. Know you are breathing out.

Ask if your thought, feeling, or perception is creating suffering
   or well-being.

Explore the contents of the thought, feeling, or perception. Allow
   its true nature to be revealed.

Ask who created this.

Answer and smile.

Ask if this thought, feeling, or perception is who you are.

Answer and smile.

Dwell in the present moment.

Sit in this contemplative exercise for 5–10 minutes.

229

Smell

An easy way to improve your outlook on life is to smell something good.

Select something with a smell you want to enjoy, like a rose, peach, or freshly baked pie.

Hold it near your nose and breathe in.

Be aware of changes in the experience of the smell as you become saturated with the odor.

Be alert to sensations in your body as you breathe the smell in and out.

After several minutes, move the item away.

After several more minutes, move the item farther away.

Stay alert to the possibility of smell and continue being aware of breathing.

Be mindful. Wake up to smell!

230

Changing focus

Experiment with gently directing your awareness from one focus to your breath.

Try to focus on one object of attention, whether it is a physical object (like a candle) or a mental object (like wanting a snack) for as long as you can.

To increase your powers of awareness, you can develop concentration on a particular object.

Once you have stabilized your concentration, you can expand your awareness.

Work with this exercise for 10–15 minutes.

231

ALTERNATE BREATHING VISUALIZATION

You can do an alternate nostril breathing as a visualization rather than a physical technique. Instead of physically holding and opening each nostril, you are simply going to imagine you are doing so.

Imagine you are inhaling up the right side of your body from your foot up to the right nostril and skull.

As you exhale, imagine you are exhaling from the top of the left side of your skull down through your left foot.

Then inhale up the left side and follow by exhaling down the right side.

This is one full cycle of alternate breathing visualization.

Do this for 10–20 cycles and then return to natural breathing for about 3 minutes with the breath moving as evenly as possibly through both sides.

232

One breath cycle

Try staying with one complete in-breath and one complete out-breath.

Keep your mind open for this full breath cycle and stay in the present moment. Let go of your ideas about getting somewhere or having something happen.

After that, try for one more breath cycle, and then maybe one more. You can repeat this for as long as you are comfortable.

When the mind wanders, return to the breath. This is a wonderful mind-training exercise for concentration and mindfulness.

Wake-up call: skillfulness

There is nothing special we have to do to eliminate unskillful mental states or to make skillful ones happen, except to be aware of the present moment. No mental state has the power to disturb the mind, unless you let it. There is nothing to be elated or depressed about. You want to develop a mind that clings to nothing, condemns nothing, and expects nothing. If there is no clinging, no condemning, no expectations of how things should be, the mind will stay clear and balanced and actions will be skillful.

233

Prepare to cook

Before you begin cooking, ritually wash and bless your hands.

Clear your mind with 3 deep breaths.

Keep in mind those people you are going to be feeding, feeling love go from your heart into the food.

After cooking, clear your mind again with 3 deep breaths and then serve the food with ceremony.

Wake-up call: sleep

Eat when hungry, sleep when tired. Simply listen to the rhythms of the body. Upon retiring, sleep as if you have entered your last sleep. Let the mind and body recharge. Upon awakening, leave your bed behind you.

234

LIFT THE SKY

This breathing exercise will help you relax and focus
your attention.

Stand with arms at your sides, eyes closed. Loosen any
bodily tension.

Take a few deep breaths through your nose, then hold for 10
before exhaling through your nose.

Inhale, raising your palms to the sky and hold for 10.

Exhale through the mouth and begin to push upward powerfully.
Mentally push the sky upward.

As you slowly inhale, bring your arms down and then up to
shoulder level at the end of the inhale.

Hold for a count of 10 and then push the sky as you exhale.

Do this exercise up to 5 breath cycles.

235

CHORE–BASED BREATHING

Try a chore-based breathing counting meditation to help you appreciate the work you are doing. This is done in conjunction with a specific task or chore you do on a daily basis—preferably something short and that you find you do rather automatically without it requiring much thought.

Simply count the breaths as you do the task.

Number each exhale and don't try to control the speed or regularity of the breath.

If thoughts intrude, just go back to counting the breath by numbering each exhale.

By simply counting the breaths, you transform a task that could be mindless into something that is more exciting and rewarding.

236

Task-based breathing

This is for quick relief when you feel overwhelmed.

Take a few seconds to relax and breathe deeply.

Accept that you cannot do everything at once. You can only do one thing at a time. Continue breathing deeply.

Decide to focus on just one task and clear your mind of everything else. Change from deep breaths to natural breathing.

Whenever your mind tries to think about other things still to be done, gently bring it back to the task at hand. Help you return to the task by focusing on your breathing.

Now focus on that one task with mindfulness. Be aware of everything about it and use all of your senses: sight, smell, touch, etc.

Calmly watch yourself doing the task until it is done.

Then move on to the next task.

237

NATURAL BREATH

For 10 minutes, lie in the relaxation pose on the ground or on a
bed, legs separated and flopped open, with your hands on your
belly to feel your natural breath.

Placing your hands on your belly helps you focus more on the
simple rise and fall of the belly as it synchronizes with the
breath. It is easier to feel exhalation fading into emptiness.
Inhalation may become smoother because you are watching
how your torso fills with breath.

When you first observe the breath, you will be seeing your
habitual breath. Note the inhibitions and restrictions that
define your habitual breath.

Move toward natural breath, a feeling like lying on the earth and
watching the clouds move through the sky.

You will start to feel a great sense of relief as your body moves into
balance and contentment.

Do this exercise for at least 10 minutes.

238

Breathing to sleep

When you have trouble sleeping or wake up in the middle of the
night and have trouble getting back to sleep, try focusing on
your breathing to bring you back to sleep.

Relax your face, then tongue and throat.

Focus on your breathing and mentally count 1 to 10 on the inhale
and exhale. Inhale 1, exhale 2, inhale 3, etc.

Continue to 10, if you are still awake.

Another way to do this exercise is on the inhalation mentally
say "falling" and on the exhalation say "asleep" until you have
arrived at sleep.

239

Sport breathing

Taking deep breaths at various times during sports practices and competition can help refocus you and improve your performance.

For example, in basketball, when you're foul shooting, stand on the line, take 3 deep breaths, and relax before you shoot.

Before your golf swing or before your putt, take 3 deep breaths.

Before you roll a bowling ball or throw a horseshoe, take 3 deep breaths.

Before you lift a barbell, take 3 deep breaths.

This breathing technique can help you get into the zone, which is extremely important when participating in sports.

240

Watching the Breath

Make sure you are comfortable, close your eyes, and focus your attention between your eyes.

Take a few deep, slow breaths.

Begin watching your breath.

Notice when you inhale and notice when you exhale.

Don't judge your breathing or try to change it. Just watch.

If your mind wanders, just bring it gently back to watching your breath.

Even a few minutes of this is relaxing and rejuvenating.

241

Full, Natural Breathing

Sit comfortably with your eyes closed.

Begin with an exhale out of your mouth.

Then inhale deeply through your nose, and hold for a second or two.

Exhale with a short burst, like blowing out a candle, then with a long, slow finish.

Completely relax your mind and body.

Repeat 3 times.

Then inhale deeply to the bottom of your spine, first filling your lungs from the bottom, to middle, to top. Hold for a moment.

Exhale slowly, emptying the lungs from the bottom, to middle, to top, gently squeezing out all the air. Hold for a moment.

Repeat this part of the exercise for 5 minutes.

242

Six-second breath

Research suggests that a rate of 10 breaths per minute is the most beneficial rate for our health. Most people breathe much faster, around 15–20 breaths per minute, faster or slower as dictated by stress and emotions such as anger, grief, and frustration.

With slower breathing, the main physiological benefit is that it increases oxygen saturation in cells, unleashing a cascade of positive effects, including giving you more energy and increased cognitive abilities.

So, here is the exercise:

Inhale deeply for 2 seconds.

Hold for 1 second.

Exhale for 2 seconds, slowly and completely to empty the lungs.

Hold for 1 second and allow oxygen to saturate the cells.

Repeat for as long as you feel comfortable. You can develop this to be the natural way you breathe. Once you have developed the habit of slow deep breathing, and your body remembers that this is the natural way to breathe, it will slowly become a part of everything that you do.

243

OBSERVING

Developing the habit of noticing changes in your breathing can become a powerful tool for you to handle stress. It takes less than 20 seconds and helps you to unconsciously monitor your breathing. Remind yourself as many times a day as you can to do this.

Stop.

Notice your breathing.

Take 2–3 slow, deep breaths.

Continue on with what you were doing. When you get into the habit of doing this simple exercise throughout the day, you train your body to breathe properly and enjoy the health benefits that come along with that.

244

Awareness reminders

You can be creative in cultivating awareness and use your breath
to do this.

Choose a reminder for the day or week and each time you see or
hear the reminder, stop and notice your breathing, taking 3
slow, deep breaths.

Examples are:
alarm on your computer calendar, cell phone, or other timing device
cell phone reminders
computer calendar
dashboard
email task list
mirror
note on the bulletin board
refrigerator
sticky note on your computer or bathroom mirror

Be creative yet practical with your choice.

Whenever you see or hear the reminder, take the 3 slow, deep
breaths before proceeding.

245

ENERGY WAVE

This exercise removes tension and gives you an energy boost. It can be done anywhere you are sitting.

Slowly inhale, progressively tensing your muscles and holding them in this order:
tense the muscles of the feet
tense the calves
tense the thighs
tense the buttocks
tense the pelvis
tense the stomach
tense the arms
tense the chest
tense the neck

Hold all these areas of the body tense for a few seconds.

Exhale and relax all the muscles in the opposite order:
relax the neck
relax the chest
relax the arms
relax the stomach
relax the pelvis
relax the buttocks
relax the thighs
relax the calves
relax the feet

Repeat the full exercise 2 more times.

Wake-up call: slowing down

Wake up in the morning and allow yourself some slow,
mindful breaths before you get out of bed. Take 3 deep
breaths before opening your laptop or answering the
phone. Choose the longest checkout line—then breathe
slowly, becoming aware of your impatience and allowing
it to dissolve. Stop criticizing too-slow sales help or
customers. Put meals in the slow cooker instead of the
microwave. Focus on one thing at a time instead of
multitasking. Take slow deep breaths while in a meeting,
in the car, or while waiting in a doctor's office. Read a
book or meditate before going to sleep.

Wake-up call: solitude

Real solitude is in the mind and should be enjoyed. If you
have little attachment and craving, you can live in solitude
in the midst of a crowd. You can let go of your sense of
possession and ownership.

246

Waterfall Breathing for Pain

Sometimes pain feels like fire. The part of your body that is in pain feels a burning sensation. The way to put out this fire is through water.

Sit comfortably with your eyes closed. Relax.

On the inhale, visualize your abdomen filling like a waterfall of cold water.

Hold.

Exhale, letting the imaginary waterfall flow to the area that is in pain, which is on fire.

Continue doing this for at least 5 minutes, feeling the fire going out as it is extinguished by the cold water.

Wake-up call: spirituality

Live a meaningful life of the spirit, one that recognizes we all will die one day. Well before the event, it is good to make peace with this inevitability. No life can be truly aware and truly fearless without such acceptance.

247

LOVELY SCENE

There are times in life when the stress is so high you just need to escape. But there is no need to travel anywhere because you can escape in your mind.

Close your eyes and imagine the place you find most peaceful and beautiful, even someplace you have not yet visited.

Visualize the details of the sun, sky, wind, water, and land.

Inhale, focusing your senses on these details. What are you seeing, hearing, smelling, touching?

Exhale, relaxing into a more pleasant body and mind state.

Your inhalation is focusing on the details of what you are seeing, hearing, smelling, and touching, while your exhalation is focusing on relaxing the body and mind.

Continue this for 10–20 minutes.

248

RELEASING PRESSURE

Pressure can build within you so much you feel like you are going to explode. This breathing exercise helps you release the rising pressure in a healthful way.

Exhale first, through your mouth.

Slowly inhale through your nose or mouth, filling your lungs from bottom to top.

Exhale for a slow count of 10, pursing your lips and letting your cheeks inflate.

Repeat for 5 minutes or longer until you feel the pressure releasing and anxiety lessening.

Wake-up call: strength

By meditating, you are strengthening aspects of your mind that are already there—like working out muscles through physical exercise. Mindfulness and awareness give the mind strength to simply be present.

249

HEALING BREATH

Lie down with your eyes closed.

Inhale and visualize your breath coming in through the top of your head. Follow it to the bottom of your stomach.

Hold your breath as a ball of energy in your stomach.

Exhale and imagine your breath as water flowing from your stomach and out through the balls of your feet. Pause briefly.

Repeat 3 times.

Then do three more versions, 3 times each.

Inhale. Hold. Exhale and visualize your breath as water coming from your stomach, up and around your spine, down your arms, and out the palms of your hands.

Inhale. Hold. Exhale and visualize your breath as water coming from your stomach, up and around your spine, up and around your head, and out through your eyes.

Inhale. Hold. Exhale and let your breath permeate your body, with it escaping out of your skin.

To complete this exercise, you should complete all 12 visualizations.

250

Breathing during exercise

This is a three-part breathing practice that would work well for walking, cycling, swimming, running, hiking, and other repetitive motion exercises. It takes practice to make a breathing system part of your exercise. You will find that slower, deeper breathing during exercise gives you more endurance and energy.

Inhale for 2 counts.

Retain the breath for 2 counts.

Exhale for 4 counts.

You can change the counts so that they are something you can maintain and the sequence feels natural to you. If your mind wanders or you lose count, gently bring your mind back to the count.

Wake-up call: taste

As you begin to eat, notice the taste of your food. Eat slowly and mindfully and enjoy tasting your food. There may be a tendency to gobble or impatience to consume as much as possible. Notice this hurriedness and slow down. Occasionally pause, put down your utensil, fold your hands, close your eyes. Really taste the food.

251

TAI CHI BREATHING

Tai chi is exercise where one focuses the mind solely on the movements of the form to help bring about a state of mental calm and clarity. Almost all tai chi movements are alternating opening and closing movements. It is best to learn tai chi in a class, from a teacher, or from an exercise video. This is basically what happens:

When your hands are apart or you step forward in tai chi, that is an opening movement.

When your hands come closer or down or you step back in tai chi, that is a closing movement.

When you are inhaling, you are taking in life energy and storing energy.

When you are exhaling, you are delivering energy or force.

When you inhale, you feel breath pull your head toward heaven.

When you exhale, you feel the "silken thread" pull down toward the earth.

To practice tai chi breathing, inhale and exhale through your nose.

Aim for a long, continuous breath without a pause, like a circle.

Breathe to and from the belly, giving your organs an internal massage.

Attention to breathing can break these patterns, letting people inhale more fresh air, smoothly and calmly.

Don't limit this type of relaxed, smooth breathing to only tai chi workouts. It's also great during normal activities throughout the day as well.

Each breath is a new opportunity to practice.

Wake-up call: thought

Acknowledge thought rather than denying it. Thoughts given control can block your creativity and ability to communicate. Engage your thoughts with a lightness and playfulness, with an attitude that they do not have power over you. Help them move along. Right thought also means thinking kindly and refusing to engage in cruel, mean, covetous, or otherwise nasty thoughts. What you think is what you are.

Wake-up call: tolerance

People who create problems for us provide us with a good opportunity to practice tolerance. The antidote to hatred is tolerance. Tolerance enables one to refrain from acting angrily to the harm inflicted on you by others. Tolerance protects you from being conquered by hatred.

252

Sunrise breath

Stand with your feet slightly apart and your arms at your sides.

Inhale deeply and drop your chin to your chest, tensing your neck and shoulders, while bringing your hands up slowly to right in front of your chest, palms up, fingertips nearly touching.

Exhale and turn your palms down, slowly pushing downward until your arms are extended, palms parallel to the floor in front of your groin, fingertips still nearly touching.

Repeat the inhale movement but this time extend the fingers up and slightly behind your head with your body arcing slightly backward, lower back and buttocks tight, and your eyes looking skyward.

Exhale as you come back to standing upright and slowly lower your arms to the starting position, relaxed by your sides.

Repeat this exercise 3 times.

253

RELEASING UPSET

Either lie down or sit comfortably in a chair.

Reach up with both hands, taking a deep breath.

Hold your breath, making tight fists and squeezing the muscles in your arms.

Exhale slowly and, arms still tensed, bring your fists down to your chest.

Repeat several times.

Then, cross your arms in front of your chest with your fingers touching the upper chest just under the shoulders, wrists crossing at the center of your chest.

Lower your chin to your chest and inhale 4 short breaths quickly through your nose, without exhaling.

Hold a few seconds.

Exhale slowly through your mouth.

Repeat this part of the exercise for 2–3 minutes.

254

Prana Breathing

Prana is the driving force behind all energy.

Sit with your back straight and breathe through your nose.

Bring your palms together over your head.

Inhale deeply through your nose, open your eyes, and bulge them out to draw in light. Visualize drawing in energy through the top of your head, face, and ears.

When your lungs are full, hold your breath. Close your eyes and concentrate on the point between your eyebrows, visualizing a bright light. Hold here for as long as comfortable.

Exhale and watch the light dissolve into a shower of energy that falls over you.

Do this from 1–10 times.

255

COUNTING BACKWARD II

Sit comfortably and breathe through your nose.

Inhale: 4, 3, 2, 1

Exhale: 4, 3, 2, 1

Inhale: 3, 2, 1

Exhale: 3, 2, 1

Inhale: 2, 1

Exhale: 2, 1

Do this 10 times and notice if you feel calmer.

Wake-up call: touch

If you are walking for a meditation, simply be aware of the touch of each step. The feeling of the impact they have on the sidewalk, grass, or trail. Then stretch out your hand and touch an object very gently and with great sensitivity. Understand the power of a touch. Rejoice in the awakening of your senses.

256

INCREASE PRANA FLOW

To increase prana (energy) flow throughout your body, do this exercise. It should feel like club soda pulsating throughout your body.

Sit and breathe through your nose.

Inhale to a count of 8 and exhale through your nose to a count of 8.

Inhale to a count of 8, visualizing prana (life energy) streaming into you as a bright light.

Hold your breath for 4 counts and see the prana circulating throughout your body.

Exhale to a count of 8, noticing negativity leaving your body.

Repeat this for as long as you like.

Wake-up call: tranquility

True happiness leads to tranquility. As the mind calms down, it naturally becomes better able to concentrate. As your concentration deepens you can proceed to train the mind toward full concentration. Rest in tranquility and you will be calm, fulfilled, and happy. Take refuge in your calm center.

257

EXTENDING EXHALATION

Sit comfortably and breathe through your nose, without pausing between inhalation and exhalation.

Exhale for 6 seconds.

Inhale for 3 seconds.

With each long exhalation, see stress leaving your system.

Continue for 1–3 minutes. Alternatively, you can exhale for 4 seconds and inhale for 2 seconds.

Wake-up call: trust

There is no better description for trust than the Serenity Prayer: God, grant me the serenity to accept the things I cannot change; courage to change the things I can; and wisdom to know the difference. Living one day at a time; Enjoying one moment at a time; Accepting hardships as the pathway to peace; Taking, as He did, this sinful world as it is, not as I would have it; Trusting that He will make all things right if I surrender to His Will; That I may be reasonably happy in this life and supremely happy with Him Forever in the next. Amen.

258

Single nostril breathing

In the morning, sit and breathe through your nose.

Close your left nostril with your right ring and little fingers.

Inhale deeply through your right nostril for a count of 4 and then exhale for a count of 8.

Repeat 10 times.

In the evening, sit and breathe through your nose.

Close your right nostril with your right thumb.

Inhale deeply through your left nostril for a count of 4 and exhale for a count of 8.

Repeat 10 times. This exercise can open the breathing passages for easier breathing.

259

SAMANA BREATHING

Samana is a term for the energy that extracts oxygen to transport it to your cells. It draws energy inward from the periphery and concentrates it in the center of your body. Samana controls the body's ability to digest food and oxygen, sensory experiences, and intellectual stimulation. When samana is healthy, we benefit from strong digestion, vitality, and balance at every level.

Sit comfortably with your legs crossed. Sit outdoors if you can. Breathe through your nose and close your eyes.

Inhale deeply through your nose, drawing breath into the belly.

Hold your breath and visualize samana energy in your solar plexus, behind the stomach, as multicolored and spiraling inward.

Exhale slowly through your nose and visualize a well of energy in your solar plexus from which you can draw nourishment for your body, mind, and spirit.

Repeat this 3–5 times.